I0416886

July 2013

# FLOOD INSURANCE

# More Information Needed on Subsidized Properties

# GAO Highlights

Highlights of GAO-13-607, a report to congressional committees

# FLOOD INSURANCE

## More Information Needed on Subsidized Properties

## Why GAO Did This Study

FEMA, which administers NFIP, estimated that in 2012 more than 1 million of its residential flood insurance policies—about 20 percent—were sold at subsidized rates; nearly all were located in high-risk flood areas. Because of their relatively high losses and lower premium rates, subsidized policies have been a financial burden on the program. Due to NFIP's financial instability and operating and management challenges, GAO placed the program on its high-risk list in 2006. The Biggert-Waters Act eliminated subsidized rates on certain properties and mandated GAO to study the remaining subsidized properties. This report examines (1) the number, location, and characteristics of properties that continue to receive subsidized rates compared with full-risk rate properties; (2) the information needed to estimate the historic cost of subsidies and establish rates for previously subsidized policies that reflect the risk of flooding; and (3) options to reduce the financial impact of remaining subsidized policies. GAO analyzed NFIP data on types of policies, premiums, and claims and publicly available home value and household income data. GAO also interviewed representatives from FEMA, insurance industry associations, and floodplain managers.

## What GAO Recommends

FEMA should develop and implement a plan to obtain flood risk information needed to determine full-risk rates for properties with previously subsidized rates. FEMA agreed with the recommendation.

View GAO-13-607. For more information, contact Alicia Puente Cackley at (202) 512-8678 or cackleya@gao.gov.

## What GAO Found

The Biggert-Waters Flood Insurance Reform Act of 2012 (Biggert-Waters Act) immediately eliminated subsidies for about 438,000 National Flood Insurance Program (NFIP) policies, but subsidies on an estimated 715,000 policies across the nation remain. Depending on factors such as policyholder behavior, the number of subsidized policies will continue to decline over time. For example, as properties are sold and the Federal Emergency Management Agency (FEMA) resolves data limitations and defines key terms, more subsidies will be eliminated. GAO analysis found that remaining subsidized policies would cover properties in every state and territory where NFIP operates, with the highest numbers in Florida, Louisiana, and California. In comparing remaining subsidized and nonsubsidized policies GAO found varying characteristics. For example, counties with the highest and lower home values had a larger percentage of subsidized versus nonsubsidized policies.

**Estimated Remaining Subsidized Policies and Percentage of Policies by State They Represent**

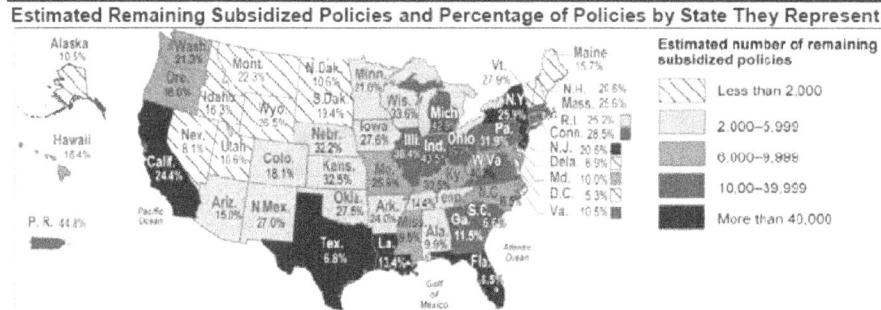

Sources: GAO analysis of FEMA data; Map Resources (map).

Data constraints limit FEMA's ability to estimate the aggregate cost of subsidies and establish rates reflecting actual flood risks on previously subsidized policies. FEMA does not have sufficient historical program data on the percentage of full-risk rates that subsidized policyholders have paid to estimate the financial impact—in terms of the difference between subsidized and full-risk premium rates—to NFIP of subsidies. Also, because not all policyholders are required to provide documentation about their flood risk, FEMA generally lacks information needed to apply full-risk rates (as required by the Biggert-Waters Act) on previously subsidized policies. FEMA is encouraging these policyholders to voluntarily submit this documentation. Federal internal control standards state that agencies should identify and analyze risks associated with achieving program objectives and develop a plan for obtaining needed data. Without this documentation, the new rates may not accurately reflect a property's full flood risk, and policyholders may be charged rates that are too high or too low relative to their risk of flooding.

Options from GAO's previous and current work for reducing the financial impact of subsidies on NFIP include (1) adjusting the pace of subsidy elimination, (2) targeting assistance or subsidies based on financial need, or (3) increasing mitigation efforts, such as relocation or elevation that reduce a property's flood risk. However, these options have advantages and disadvantages. Moreover, the options are not mutually exclusive, and combining them could help offset some disadvantages.

_____ United States Government Accountability Office

# Contents

Figures

**Abbreviations**

| | |
|---|---|
| ACS | American Community Survey |
| FEMA | Federal Emergency Management Agency |
| FIRM | Flood Insurance Rate Map |
| NFIP | National Flood Insurance Program |
| SFHA | Special Flood Hazard Area |
| WYO | Write-Your-Own |
| ASFPM | Association of State Floodplain Managers |
| PwC | PricewaterhouseCoopers |

This is a work of the U.S. government and is not subject to copyright protection in the United States. The published product may be reproduced and distributed in its entirety without further permission from GAO. However, because this work may contain copyrighted images or other material, permission from the copyright holder may be necessary if you wish to reproduce this material separately.

**GAO** U.S. GOVERNMENT ACCOUNTABILITY OFFICE

441 G St. N.W.
Washington, DC 20548

July 3, 2013

The Honorable Tim Johnson
Chairman
The Honorable Mike Crapo
Ranking Member
Committee on Banking, Housing and Urban Affairs
United States Senate

The Honorable Jeb Hensarling
Chairman
The Honorable Maxine Waters
Ranking Member
Committee on Financial Services
House of Representatives

In 2012, the Federal Emergency Management Agency (FEMA), which administers the National Flood Insurance Program (NFIP), collected $3.5 billion in premiums. It estimated that about 1.1 million of 5.5 million NFIP policies—about 20 percent—were sold at highly discounted rates that did not fully reflect the actual risk of flooding. The National Flood Insurance Act of 1968 authorized subsidized rates to encourage participation in NFIP, especially for properties in high-risk locations that otherwise would have been charged higher premiums and were built before Flood Insurance Rate Maps (FIRM) became available and the level of risk was clearly understood. The discounted premiums help achieve the goal of promoting participation in the program, but do not contribute sufficient revenues to cover potential losses. We have previously found that because of their relatively high losses and lower premium rates compared with policies that are charged rates intended to reflect the actual risk of flooding (full-risk rates), the policies receiving subsidized rates have been a financial burden on NFIP.[1]

Since 2000, NFIP has experienced several years with catastrophic losses—losses exceeding $1 billion—and has needed to borrow money

---

[1]GAO, *Flood Insurance: Options for Addressing the Financial Impact of Subsidized Premium Rates on the National Flood Insurance Program*, GAO-09-20 (Washington, D.C.: Nov. 14, 2008).

GAO-13-607 Flood Insurance

from the U.S. Treasury (Treasury) to cover claims in some years.[2] The losses resulting from Superstorm Sandy, which caused extensive damage in several states on the eastern coast of the United States in October 2012, also are expected to be catastrophic. As of May 2013, FEMA owed Treasury $24 billion—up from $17.8 billion prior to Superstorm Sandy—and had not repaid any principal on its loans since 2010. As a result of the program's importance, level of indebtedness to Treasury, substantial financial exposure for the federal government and taxpayers, and FEMA's management challenges, NFIP has been on our high-risk list since 2006.[3] In other reports, we also have identified a number of management and operational challenges that have hindered FEMA's ability to effectively administer NFIP.[4]

The Biggert-Waters Flood Insurance Reform Act of 2012 (Biggert-Waters Act) introduced many changes intended to strengthen the future solvency of NFIP.[5] In particular, the act eliminated subsidized premium rates for several types of properties.[6] In addition to program changes, the Biggert-Waters Act mandated that GAO conduct a number of studies, including this study on the properties that continue to receive subsidized rates after the implementation of the act and options to further reduce these subsidies.[7]

---

[2]FEMA has authority to borrow money from the U.S. Treasury to pay losses that exceed premium revenue and any accumulated surplus. Before Superstorm Sandy, this borrowing authority stood at $20.725 billion. In January 2013, Congress passed and the President signed into law a $9.7 billion increase in this authority to pay flood claims related to Superstorm Sandy. This raised FEMA's borrowing authority to $30.425 billion. Pub. L. No. 113-1, 127 Stat. 3 (Jan. 6, 2013).

[3]See GAO, FEMA: Action Needed to Improve Administration of the National Flood Insurance Program, GAO-11-297 (Washington, D.C.: June 9, 2011; High-Risk Program, GAO-06-497T (Washington, D.C.: Mar. 15, 2006); and High-Risk Series: An Update, GAO-13-359T (Washington, D.C.: Feb. 13, 2013).

[4]See GAO, National Flood Insurance Program: Continued Actions Needed to Address Financial and Operational Issues, GAO-10-1063T (Washington, D.C.: Sept. 22, 2010); GAO-11-297; and Flood Insurance: FEMA's Rate-Setting Process Warrants Attention, GAO-09-12 (Washington, D.C.: Oct. 31, 2008).

[5]Pub. L. No. 112-141, Div. F, Title II, Subtit. A, 126 Stat. 405, 916 (July 6, 2012).

[6]Pub. L. No. 112-141, §100205, classified as amended at 42 U.S.C. 4014(a)(2) and (g).

[7]Pub. L. No. 112-141, §100231.

This report discusses (1) the number, location, and financial characteristics of properties that continue to receive subsidized rates compared with full-risk rate properties; (2) the information needed to estimate the historic cost of subsidies and establish rates for previously subsidized policies that reflect the risk of flooding; and (3) options to reduce the financial impact of remaining subsidized properties.

To address these objectives, we analyzed FEMA data on NFIP flood insurance policies, claims, and repetitive losses, as well as historic data on claims and premiums for policies with subsidized and full-risk rates.[8] We used the data and information from FEMA officials about their plans to implement the Biggert-Waters Act to determine which policies would retain subsidized rates. We determined the number, location, and coverage amounts of these remaining subsidized policies, the claims and premiums attributable to them, and the historic frequency with which they exited the program. For requested information on the financial characteristics of policies that was not available from FEMA, we used indicators from publicly available census and real estate data as well as NFIP policy-level coverage amount data. We used these data to analyze the similarities and differences in the financial characteristics of properties with subsidized and full-risk rates. For example, we ranked nationwide county-level median home value and median household income from the 2007 through 2011 5-year American Community Survey (ACS)—a continuous survey of households conducted by the U.S. Census Bureau.[9] We determined the relative ranking for counties with large numbers of remaining subsidized policies. We also selected five case study counties to illustrate similarities and differences in characteristics of policies at the city level within these counties. Results from these case studies cannot be projected nationwide. We selected the counties based on the number of relevant NFIP policies, location, and reliability of publicly available real estate data for the county. We also used the publicly available real estate data on median home values for cities in these counties. We assessed the reliability of each data source we used by interviewing agency officials and gathering and analyzing available information about how the data

---

[8]The scope of this report excludes policies with grandfathered rates and policies with preferred risk premiums, which are also discounted.

[9]The 2007 through 2011 ACS 5-year estimates are based on multiyear period estimates for the years 2007 through 2011 and should not be interpreted as estimates for any particular year in that period.

were collected and maintained and performed electronic tests of required data elements. We also spoke with representatives from a private company that collects and estimates data on real estate values as well as with an academic and other users of these publicly available real estate data about the reliability of the data. We determined that the data from each source we used were sufficiently reliable for the purposes of this report. We analyzed NFIP's legislative history and relied on FEMA's interpretation and implementation of legislative requirements authorizing subsidized rates for certain properties in high-risk locations. We interviewed representatives of NFIP, the insurance industry, and floodplain managers. Finally, we spoke with an academic about a study of NFIP properties and analyzed other studies on relevant flood insurance issues. See appendix I for more details about our scope and methodology.

We conducted this performance audit from September 2012 to July 2013 in accordance with generally accepted government auditing standards. Those standards require that we plan and perform the audit to obtain sufficient, appropriate evidence to provide a reasonable basis for our findings and conclusions based on our audit objectives. We believe that the evidence obtained provides a reasonable basis for our findings and conclusions based on our audit objectives.

## Background

Since the inception of NFIP in 1968, FEMA has sought to have local communities adopt floodplain management ordinances and offered flood insurance to their residents in an effort to reduce the need for government assistance after a flood. Premium subsidies were seen as a way to achieve the program's objectives by ensuring that owners of existing properties in flood zones could afford flood insurance. NFIP has three components: (1) the provision of flood insurance; (2) the requirement that participating communities adopt and enforce floodplain management regulations; and (3) the identification and mapping of floodplains. Community participation in NFIP is voluntary. However, communities must join NFIP and adopt FEMA-approved building standards and floodplain management strategies in order for their residents to purchase flood insurance through the program. Additionally, communities with Special Flood Hazard Areas (SFHA)—areas at high risk for flooding—must participate in NFIP to be eligible for any form of disaster assistance loans or grants for acquisition or construction purposes in connection with a flood. Participating communities can receive discounts on flood insurance if they establish floodplain management programs that go beyond the minimum requirements of NFIP.[10] FEMA can suspend communities that do not comply with the program, and communities can withdraw from the program. As of May 2013, about 22,000 communities voluntarily participate in NFIP.[11]

Potential policyholders can purchase flood insurance that covers both buildings and contents for residential and commercial properties. NFIP's maximum coverage limit for single-family residential policyholders is $250,000 per unit for buildings and $100,000 per unit for contents. For commercial policyholders, the maximum coverage is $500,000 per unit for buildings and $500,000 for contents.

Current law prohibits federally regulated lenders, federal agency lenders, and government-sponsored enterprises for housing from making loans for real estate in SFHAs where the community is participating in NFIP, unless the property is covered by flood insurance.[12] For structures deemed not to be in SFHAs—that is, that have moderate to low risk of flooding—the purchase of flood insurance is voluntary.

## Flood Zone Designations

NFIP studies and maps flood risks, assigning flood zone designations from high to low depending on the risk of flooding. SFHAs are high-risk areas that have a 1 percent or greater annual chance of flooding and are designated as zones A, AE, V, or VE (table 1). Areas designated as V or VE are located along the coast. Areas with a moderate-to-low risk for flooding are designated as zones B, C, or X. Areas where analysis of the flood risk has not been conducted are designated as D zones.

---

[10]To be eligible for these discounts, communities must participate in the Community Rating System, a voluntary program established in 1990 to encourage community floodplain management activities that exceed the minimum NFIP standards. Under the Community Rating System, flood insurance premium rates are discounted to reward community actions that meet three goals: (1) reduce flood damage to insurable property, (2) strengthen and support the insurance aspects of NFIP, and (3) encourage a comprehensive approach to floodplain management.

[11]Not all participating NFIP communities have residents or businesses with policies.

[12]42 U.S.C § 4012a. Flood insurance on properties that do not have a mortgage in these areas is voluntary.

GAO-13-607 Flood Insurance

**Table 1: National Flood Insurance Program Flood Zone Designations**

| Designations | Risk level |
| --- | --- |
| Flood zones B, C, X | Moderate- to low-risk |
| Flood zones A, AE | Special Flood Hazard Area—High-risk |
| Flood zones V, VE | Special Flood Hazard Area—High-risk coastal |
| Flood zone D | Undetermined risk |

Source: FEMA.

## Subsidized Premium Rates

NFIP offers two types of flood insurance premiums: subsidized and full-risk. Subsidized rates are not based on actual flood risk. According to FEMA, subsidized rates represent only about 40 percent to 45 percent of rates that reflect full flood risk. (We discuss how FEMA determines rates in more detail later in this report.) The type of policy and the subsequent rate a policyholder pays depend on several property characteristics—for example, whether the structure was built before or after a community's FIRM had been issued and the location of the structure in the floodplain. Structures built after a community's FIRM was published must be built to meet FEMA building standards and pay full-risk rates. Some communities may implement activities that exceed the minimum standards.

Prior to the Biggert-Waters Act, subsidized policies accounted for about 21 percent of all NFIP policies, while those with full-risk premiums accounted for the remaining 79 percent. While the percentage of subsidized policies has decreased since the program was established, the number of these policies has stayed fairly constant (see fig. 1).

Figure 1: Number of Total NFIP Policies and Number and Percentage of Subsidized Policies, 1978-2012

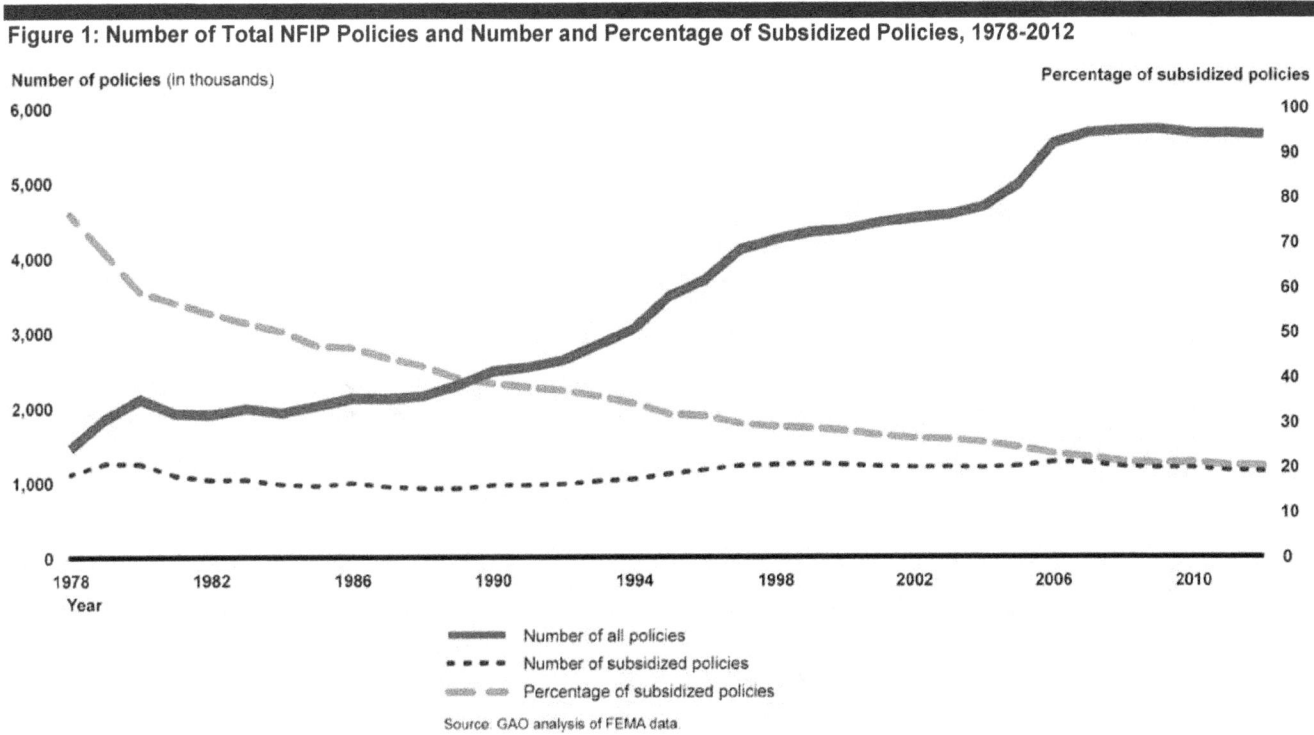

As communities were mapped and joined NFIP, new subsidized policies were added. As shown in figure 2, the percentage change in subsidized policies generally followed the same trend as the percentage change in total policies.

**Figure 2: Percentage Change in Subsidized and Total NFIP Policies, 1978-2012**

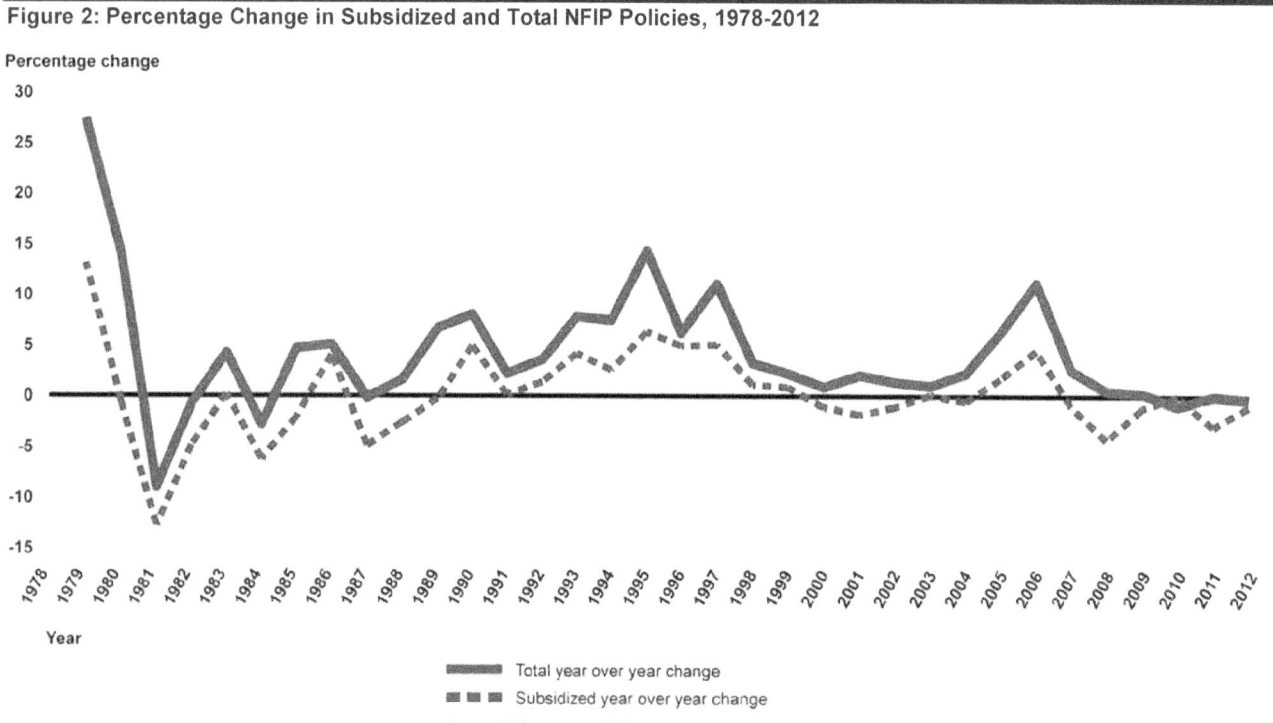

Total year over year change

■ ■ ■ Subsidized year over year change

Source GAO analysis of FEMA data

Even with highly discounted rates, subsidized premiums are, on average, higher than full-risk premiums. The premiums are higher because subsidized pre-FIRM structures generally are more prone to flooding (that is, riskier) than other structures. In general, pre-FIRM properties were not constructed according to the program's building standards or were built without regard to base flood elevation—the level relative to mean sea level at which there is a 1 percent or greater chance of flooding in a given year. For example, the average annual subsidized premium with October 2011 rates for pre-FIRM subsidized properties located in zone A was about $1,200, while the average annual premium for post-FIRM properties in the same zone paying full-risk rates was about $500. Post-FIRM structures have been built to flood-resistant building codes or mitigation steps have been taken to reduce flood risks; thus, they are generally less flood-prone than pre-FIRM properties.[13]

## Legislative Authority for and Changes to NFIP

The authority for subsidized rates was included in the National Flood Insurance Act of 1968 as an incentive for communities to join the program by adopting and enforcing floodplain management ordinances that would reduce future flood losses. Subsidies were intended to be only part of an interim solution to long-term adjustments in land use. Congress also authorized the use of subsidized premiums because charging rates that fully and accurately reflected flood risk would be a burden to some property owners. Table 2 shows the sources of legislative authority for various subsidized premium rates.

**Table 2: Statutory Authority for NFIP Subsidized Rates, as of July 6, 2012**

| Type of property with subsidy | Definition/Description | Statute |
|---|---|---|
| Pre-FIRM A zone | Properties with unknown elevations relative to the base flood elevation in high-risk areas that were built before 1974 or before the effective date of a community's FIRM. | Sections 1307 and 1308 of the National Flood Insurance Act of 1968, as amended.[a] |
| Levees (AR and A99 zones) | Properties behind unfinished or de-certified levees (zones A99 and AR, respectively). In both cases FEMA has determined that the community is close to finishing/repairing the levee. | The National Flood Insurance Act of 1968 as added by section 816(b) of the Housing and Community Development Act of 1974, as amended.[b] The National Flood Insurance Act of 1968 as added by section 928 of the Housing and Community Development Act of 1992, as amended.[c] |
| Post-FIRM D zone | Properties with undetermined, but possible, flood hazards that were built after 1974 or the effective date of the community's FIRM. | Sections 1307 and 1308 of the National Flood Insurance Act of 1968, as amended.[d] |
| Pre-FIRM V zone | Properties located in Special Flood Hazard Areas without water surface elevations determined and with velocity that were built before FIRMs became available. | Sections 1307 and 1308 of the National Flood Insurance Act of 1968, as amended.[e] |

[13]Steps taken to reduce flood risk are known as mitigation. According to FEMA, the key mitigation steps for residential properties are elevating a building to or above the area's base flood elevation, relocating the building to an area of lower flood risk, or demolishing the building and turning the property into green space. A community also can take steps to reduce flood risk to an area by diverting the flow of water through well-designed channels and retaining walls, or by containing the water through ponds.

| Type of property with subsidy | Definition/Description | Statute |
|---|---|---|
| Post-FIRM V zone | Properties in coastal high-hazard areas built between 1975 and 1981 to be compliant with NFIP building code standards at the time, but that were grandfathered into rates when building code standards changed in 1981. | Section 1307 of the National Flood Insurance Act of 1968, as amended.[f] |
| Emergency Flood Insurance Program | Properties in communities participating in the Emergency Flood Insurance Program. The emergency program is a community's initial phase of participation in NFIP and is intended to provide a first layer amount of insurance at subsidized rates on all insurable properties before the effective date of the initial FIRM. | The National Flood Insurance Act of 1968 as added by section 408 of the Housing and Urban Development Act of 1969, as amended.[g] |

Source: GAO analysis of applicable laws.

[a]Classified at 42 U.S.C. §§ 4014(a)(2) and 4015(a).

[b]Classified at 42 U.S.C. § 4014(e).

[c]Classified at 42 U.S.C. § 4014(f).

[d]Classified at 42 U.S.C. § 4014(a)(2) but limited by 42 U.S.C. 4015(c)(1).

[e]Classified at 42 U.S.C. §§ 4014(a)(2) and 4015(a).

[f]Classified at 42 U.S.C. § 4014(a)(2) but limited by 42 U.S.C. 4015(c).

[g]Classified at 42 U.S.C. § 4056.

Since NFIP was established, Congress has enacted legislation to strengthen certain aspects of the program. The Flood Disaster Protection Act of 1973 made the purchase of flood insurance mandatory for properties in SFHAs that are secured by mortgages from federally regulated lenders. This requirement expanded the overall number of insured properties, including those that qualified for subsidized premiums. The National Flood Insurance Reform Act of 1994 expanded the purchase requirement for federally backed mortgages on properties located in an SFHA. The Bunning-Bereuter-Blumenauer Flood Insurance Reform Act of 2004 established a pilot program to mitigate properties that continually suffered from severe repeated flood losses and offer grants for properties with repetitive insurance claims.[14] Owners of these "repetitive loss" properties who refuse to accept any offer for mitigation actions face higher premiums.

---

[14]Pub. L. No. 108-264, §§ 102, 104, 118 Stat. 712, 714, 722 (June 30, 2004).

More recently, in July 2012, Congress passed the Biggert-Waters Act.[15] The act extended the authorization for NFIP for 5 years and made reforms to NFIP that include eliminating existing subsidies for

- any residential property which is not a primary residence;
- any severe repetitive loss property;[16]
- any property that has incurred flood-related damage in which the cumulative amounts of payments under this title equaled or exceeded the fair market value of such property;
- any business property; and
- any property that has experienced or sustained substantial damage exceeding 50 percent of the fair market value or substantial improvement exceeding 30 percent of the fair market value.[17]

Rates that fully reflect flood risk for the types of properties listed previously are to be phased in over several years—with increases of 25 percent each year—until the average risk premium rate for such properties is equal to the average of the risk premium rates for properties within any single risk classification.

Furthermore, according to the Biggert-Waters Act, other properties will no longer qualify for subsidies under the following circumstances:

- any NFIP policy that has lapsed in coverage, as a result of the deliberate choice of the policyholder; and
- any prospective insured who refuses to accept any offer for mitigation assistance (including an offer to relocate) following a major disaster.[18]

---

[15]Pub. L. No. 112-141, Div. F, Tit. II, Subtit. A, 126 Stat. 405, 916 (July 6, 2012).

[16]For single-family properties, such properties have incurred at least four NFIP claim payments exceeding $5,000 each, with the cumulative amount of such claims payments exceeding $20,000; or at least two separate claims have been made with the cumulative amount of the claims exceeding the value of the property. For multifamily properties, FEMA will define the term by regulation.

[17]Pub. L. No. 112-141, §100205, classified as amended at 42 U.S.C. 4014(a)(2).

[18]Pub. L. No. 112-141, §100205, classified as amended at 42 U.S.C. 4014(g)(3) and (4).

The act also stated that no new subsidies would be provided to

- any property not insured by NFIP as of the date the act was enacted; and
- any property purchased after the date of enactment of the act. (Thus, property sales trigger elimination of subsidies.)[19]

The Biggert-Waters Act also requires FEMA to adjust rates to accurately reflect the current risk of flood to properties when an area's flood map is changed, subject to any other statutory provision in chapter 50 of Title 42 of the United States Code. FEMA is determining how this provision will affect properties that were "grandfathered" into lower rates. In addition, the act allows insurance premium rate increases of 20 percent annually (previously capped at 10 percent), establishes minimum deductibles, and requires FEMA to include the losses from catastrophic years in determining premiums that are based upon "average historical loss year." It also incorporates a definition of "severe repetitive loss property" for single-family properties and required FEMA to establish a reserve fund, among other things.

## Most Subsidized Policies Continue to Receive Discounted Rates and Have Mixed Characteristics Relative to Financial Indicators

The Biggert-Waters Act eliminated subsidies on approximately 438,000 policies, and with the continuing implementation of the act, more of the subsidies on the approximately 715,000 remaining policies are expected to be eliminated over time. In terms of characteristics, the geographic distribution of remaining subsidized policies was similar to the distribution of all NFIP policies. Other characteristics we analyzed—indicators of home value and owner income—were different for the policies that continue to qualify for subsidized premium rates compared to those with full-risk rates. In particular, counties with higher home values and income levels tended to have larger percentages of remaining subsidized policies compared to those with full-risk rates.

---

[19]Pub. L. No. 112-141, §100205, classified as amended at 42 U.S.C. 4014(g)(1) and (2).

## Most Policies Estimated to Still Qualify for Subsidized Rates, but their Numbers Are Expected to Decline over Time

We estimated that the Biggert-Waters Act eliminated subsidies for approximately 438,000 policies, and that about 715,000 policies continue to qualify for subsidized premium rates (remaining subsidized policies). Before the act, subsidized policies represented about 21 percent of all policies and nearly all subsidized policies were in the high risk areas.[20] After the initial reduction of subsidies, the approximately 715,000 policies that would continue to receive subsidized rates represent about 13 percent of all NFIP policies and 21 percent of all SFHA policies.[21] The elimination affected various property types, including nonprimary residences, businesses, and severe repetitive loss properties. About 92 percent of the projected remaining subsidized policies cover single-unit primary residence properties and more than 99 percent cover properties in SFHA areas. The continuing implementation of the act is expected to decrease the number of subsidized policies. However, FEMA faces a number of implementation challenges and elimination of subsidies as required by the act will likely take years.

### Subsidy Elimination by Property Types

As mandated by the Biggert-Waters Act, FEMA has begun phasing out subsidized premiums for business properties, residential properties that are not primary residences, and single-family (1-4 units) severe repetitive loss properties.[22] According to our analysis of NFIP data, the 438,000 policies that would no longer qualify for subsidized premium rates included about 345,000 nonprimary residential policies, about 87,000 business policies, and about 9,000 single-family severe-repetitive loss policies.[23] Nearly all subsidized policies for primary residential properties continue to have subsidized rates. Figure 3 summarizes our analysis of the immediate decreases in subsidized policies stemming from the act, by property type.

---

[20]Before the act, subsidized policies represented about 34 percent of all SFHA policies (33 percent of all A-zone policies and 52 percent of all V-zone policies).

[21]Policy owners that no longer qualify for subsidized rates will begin paying higher premiums, however it will take several years of increases before they are paying full-risk rates.

[22]Pub. L. No. 112-141, §100205(a)(1).

[23]Because there is some overlap among categories, the numbers do not sum to 438,000.

Figure 3: Estimated Decreases in NFIP Subsidized Policies Due to the Biggert-Waters Act, by Property Type, as of June 2012

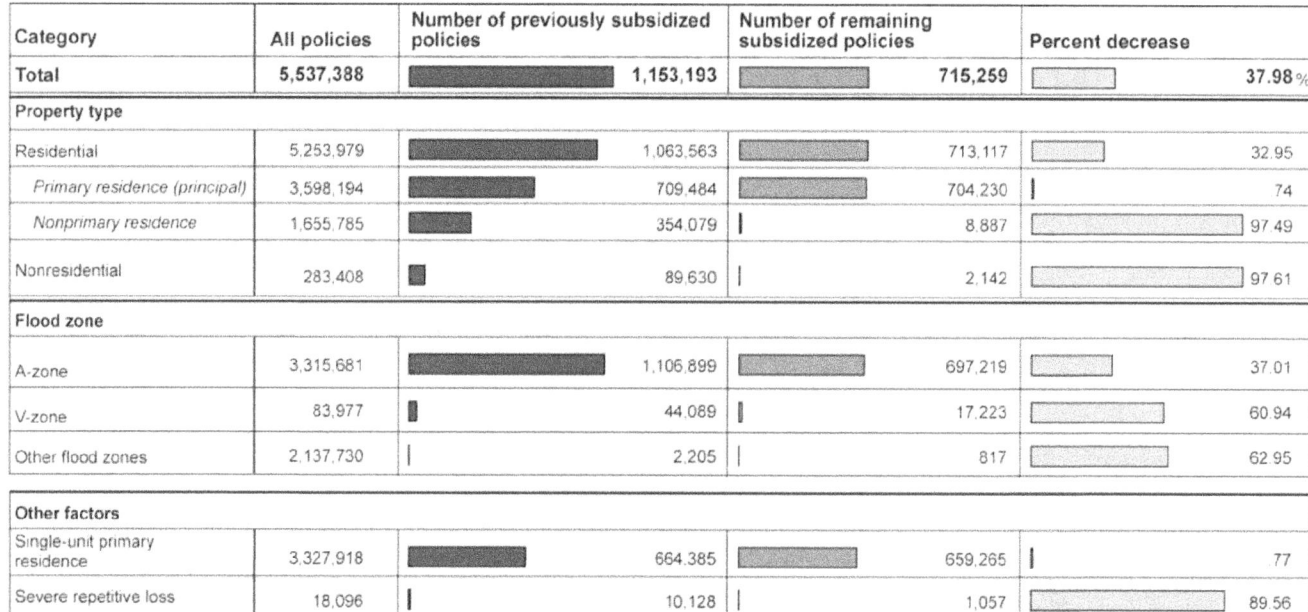

| Category | All policies | Number of previously subsidized policies | | Number of remaining subsidized policies | | Percent decrease | |
|---|---|---|---|---|---|---|---|
| Total | 5,537,388 | | 1,153,193 | | 715,259 | | 37.98% |
| **Property type** | | | | | | | |
| Residential | 5,253,979 | | 1,063,563 | | 713,117 | | 32.95 |
| *Primary residence (principal)* | 3,598,194 | | 709,484 | | 704,230 | | 74 |
| *Nonprimary residence* | 1,655,785 | | 354,079 | | 8,887 | | 97.49 |
| Nonresidential | 283,408 | | 89,630 | | 2,142 | | 97.61 |
| **Flood zone** | | | | | | | |
| A-zone | 3,315,681 | | 1,106,899 | | 697,219 | | 37.01 |
| V-zone | 83,977 | | 44,089 | | 17,223 | | 60.94 |
| Other flood zones | 2,137,730 | | 2,205 | | 817 | | 62.95 |
| **Other factors** | | | | | | | |
| Single-unit primary residence | 3,327,918 | | 664,385 | | 659,265 | | 77 |
| Severe repetitive loss | 18,096 | | 10,128 | | 1,057 | | 89.56 |

Source: GAO analysis of FEMA data.

Note: This analysis assumes that most nonresidential subsidies would be eliminated and that only the subsidies for severe repetitive loss policies defined as such in the act would be eliminated. FEMA data on the status or category of certain properties may not be current. In addition, FEMA separates out policies on condominiums, whereas we included them in the primary and nonprimary categories. Thus, our estimates could vary from FEMA's results. Further, there is some overlap in these categories and the residential and nonresidential categories do not add up to the total number of policies because the information in FEMA's database designating policies as residential or nonresidential was invalid for one policy.

## Continuing Decline in Subsidized Policies

Subsidies on most of the approximately 715,000 remaining subsidized policies should be eliminated over time. Under provisions of the Biggert-Waters Act, most policies no longer qualify for subsidies if NFIP coverage lapsed or the properties were sold or substantially damaged.[24] We estimated that with implementation of the changes in the act addressing sales and coverage lapses, the number of subsidized policies could decline by almost 14 percent per year (see fig. 4). At this rate, the number of subsidized policies would be reduced by 50 percent in approximately 5 years. After about 14 years, fewer than 100,000 subsidized policies would

---

[24]Substantially damaged is defined as damage exceeding 50 percent of the fair market value of the property.

remain. We based our estimate of the annual decline rate on the average experience of the last 10 years of NFIP data using policies with similar characteristics, but the actual outcomes and time required for subsidies to be reduced could vary. For example, the average annual decline rate for the most recent 3 years of NFIP data was about 11 percent. At this rate, the number of subsidized policies would be reduced by 50 percent in approximately 7 years, and after 18 years, fewer than 100,000 subsidized policies would remain. Additionally, changes from the act may affect the behavior of policyholders. For example, policyholders might not allow their coverage to lapse if they knew that they would lose their subsidy or they might not be able to sell their properties at the same rate if the flood insurance was more expensive.[25]

**Figure 4: Estimated Number of NFIP Remaining Subsidized Policies Using Varying Annual Decline Rates**

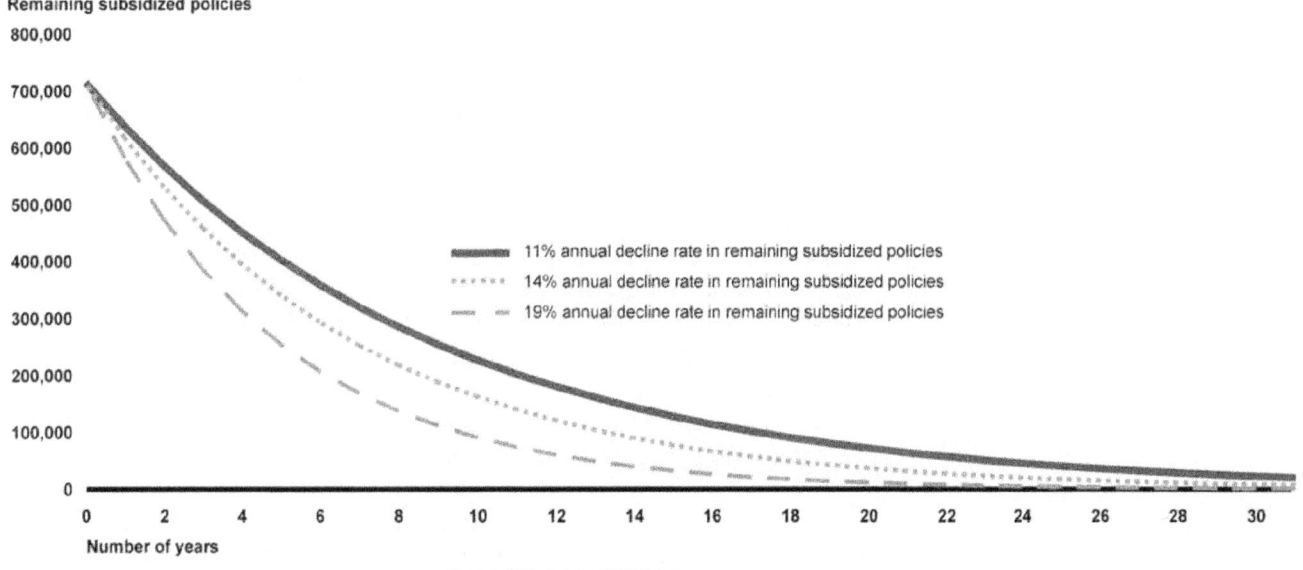

Remaining subsidized policies

Source: GAO analysis of FEMA data

[25]We compared our results with existing literature. See Erwann Michel-Kerjan, Sabine Lemoyne de Forges, and Howard Kunreuther, "Policy Tenure Under the U.S. National Flood Insurance Program (NFIP)," *Risk Analysis*, 32, no. 4 (April 2012). This study looked at policy tenure rather than decline. We compared our results to this study's results by calculating the average decline rate from their published tenure duration results. Our analysis showed about a 5 percent slower decline rate than this study. The difference was due in part to the data differences. We were able to determine when policyholders changed insurance carriers whereas these data were not available for the tenure study.

Note: We used a 13.80 percent decline rate based on analysis of 10 years of historic NFIP policy data, a 10.86 percent decline rate based on the 3 most recent years of the NFIP policy data, and an 18.66 percent decline rate based on calculations of data from Michel-Kerjan et al. study (2012).

## Implementation Challenges

The Biggert-Waters Act will likely require several years for FEMA to fully implement. FEMA officials acknowledged that they have data limitations and other issues to resolve before eliminating some subsidies. We projected that subsidies on most of the policies required to be eliminated by the act could be identified in FEMA's data; however, data limitations make implementation of some provisions of the act more difficult. For example, the act eliminated subsidies for residential policies that covered nonprimary residences. FEMA has data on whether a policy covers a primary residence but officials stated that it may be outdated or incorrect. In the past, FEMA did not collect this information for policy renewal so it may have changed over time. The act also eliminated subsidies for business policies. However, FEMA categorizes policies as residential and nonresidential rather than residential and business. As a result, FEMA does not have the information to identify nonresidential properties, such as schools or churches that are not businesses and continue to qualify for a subsidy. Beginning in October 2013, FEMA will require applicants to provide residential and business status for new policies and renewals.

Additionally, the act states that subsidies will be eliminated for policies that have received cumulative payment amounts for flood-related damage that equaled or exceeded the fair market value of the property, and for policies that experience damage exceeding 50 percent of the fair market value of the property after enactment. Currently, FEMA is unable to make this determination as it does not maintain data on the fair market value of properties insured by subsidized policies. FEMA officials said that they are in the process of identifying a data source.

FEMA will have to determine how to apply certain provisions of the Biggert-Waters Act before eliminating some subsidies. For example, the act eliminates subsidies for severe repetitive loss policies and provides a definition of severe repetitive loss for single-family homes. However, it requires FEMA to define severe repetitive loss for multifamily properties. FEMA has not yet developed this definition and we estimate that 1,000 multifamily severe repetitive loss policies will continue to receive a subsidy until the definition is developed and applied.[26] The act also

---

[26]We based this estimate on FEMA data which uses a previous definition of severe repetitive loss.

eliminates subsidies when properties are purchased. However, FEMA has not yet determined how to apply this provision of the act to condominium associations. Finally, FEMA officials stated that they have been applying the provisions of the act that eliminate subsidies only to pre-FIRM policies. As a result, approximately 5,500 subsidized post-FIRM V zone structures built before 1981 that currently receive subsidized rates would continue to qualify for subsidies.[27]

## Similarities and Differences between Properties with Subsidized versus Full-Risk Rates

We analyzed a number of characteristics of the remaining subsidized policies. First, they had a geographic distribution similar to all NFIP policies. Second, while higher percentages of remaining subsidized policies than policies with full-risk rates were found in counties with higher median home values, remaining subsidized policies generally carried smaller amounts of coverage. Third, counties with the highest median household incomes and counties at the lower end of our income ranking had larger percentages of remaining subsidized policies compared to the percentage of policies with full-risk rates. We limited our analysis of the similarities and differences between remaining subsidized policies and the policies with full-risk rates (nonsubsidized) to single-unit primary residences in SFHAs.[28]

### Location

Our analysis of NFIP data on the location of properties that would continue to receive subsidized rates shows that remaining subsidized policies would cover properties in every state and territory in which NFIP operates. Florida (133,000), Louisiana (65,000), California (64,000), New Jersey (48,000), Texas (44,000), and New York (43,000) had the highest numbers of remaining subsidized policies. These states with the addition of South Carolina also had the highest number of total NFIP policies. In contrast, Indiana, Michigan, and Puerto Rico had the highest percentages of remaining subsidized policies as a fraction of total NFIP policies in the state, representing more than 40 percent of all NFIP policies in those states. Figure 5 shows the estimated number of remaining subsidized policies by state and the remaining subsidized policies as a percentage of total NFIP policies in the state.

---

[27]According to FEMA documentation, because the previously compliant construction would be subject to very high rates if held to the later standards, discussions with Congress led to the decision to charge 1975 through 1981 construction with less than the full-risk premium rates.

[28]About 92 percent of the projected remaining subsidized policies cover single-unit primary residence properties and more than 99 percent cover properties in SFHA areas.

**Figure 5: Numbers of Estimated Remaining Subsidized Policies and the Percentage of NFIP Policies, by State, They Represent, as of June 2012**

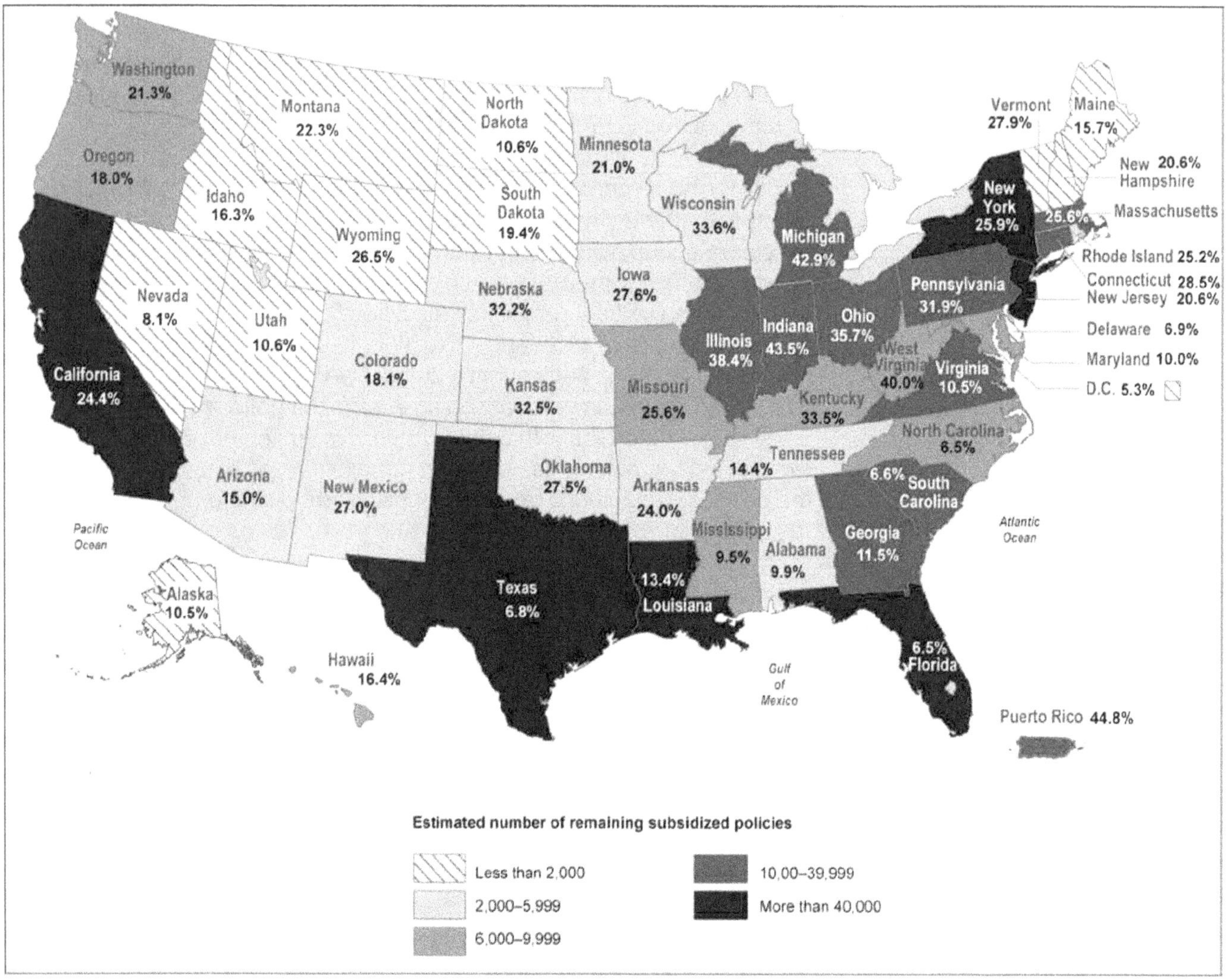

Estimated number of remaining subsidized policies

| | |
|---|---|
| Less than 2,000 | 10,00–39,999 |
| 2,000–5,999 | More than 40,000 |
| 6,000–9,999 | |

Sources: GAO analysis of FEMA data, Map Resources (map).

States with the highest percentage of remaining subsidized policies did not necessarily have the highest percentage of total NFIP policies. Some states had a higher percentage of remaining subsidized policies than the percentage of total NFIP policies in the state (see fig. 6). For example, California had 9 percent of all remaining subsidized policies and about 5 percent of all NFIP policies, and New York had 6 percent of all remaining subsidized policies and 3 percent of all policies. Other states had a larger percentage of total NFIP policies than subsidized policies. For example, Florida had 37 percent of total NFIP policies and about 19 percent of all remaining subsidized policies and Texas had about 12 percent of all policies and 6 percent of remaining subsidized policies.

**Figure 6: Percentage of All NFIP and Remaining Subsidized Policies by Selected States, June 2012**

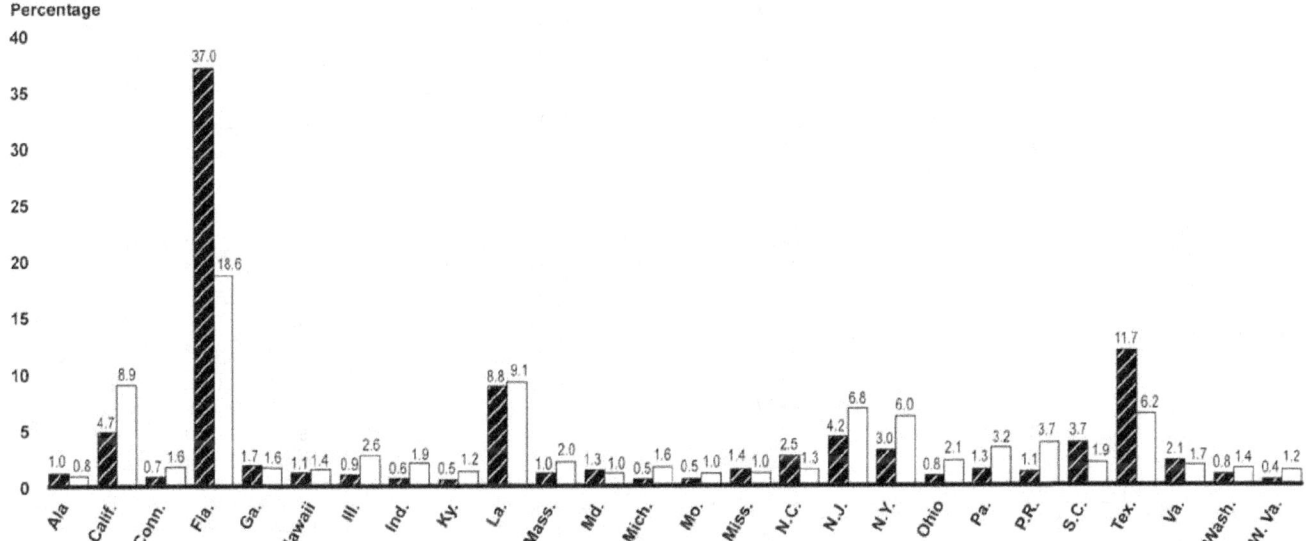

Sources: GAO analysis of FEMA data.

Note: States not listed had less than 1 percent of all NFIP policies and remaining subsidized policies.

When analyzed by county, the remaining subsidized policies were located in about 2,930 of the more than 3,100 counties with NFIP policies. The number of remaining subsidized policies in the counties varied greatly. We estimated that 151 counties had only one remaining subsidized policy, and another 1,137 had fewer than 25 remaining subsidized policies. We also estimated that 247 counties had more than 500 of these policies. Ten of these counties had more than 10,000 remaining subsidized policies, 4 of which were in Florida, 2 in Louisiana, and 1 each in California, New Jersey, New York, and Texas. Pinellas County, Florida, had the highest number of estimated remaining subsidized policies at more than 28,000.

GAO-13-607 Flood Insurance

Home Value

Counties with the highest median home values tended to have a higher percentage of remaining subsidized policies than nonsubsidized policies. For our analysis of the financial characteristics of remaining subsidized and nonsubsidized policies, we selected 351 counties that represented more than 78 percent of remaining subsidized policies.[29] See appendix II for more information about the 351 counties we selected for our analysis. Because FEMA lacks data on home values, we used several indicators of home value to compare properties in these counties that would continue to receive subsidized rates with properties charged full-risk rates (see table 3). Most of the policies were in the counties with relatively high home values. For example, the median home value for more than half of the selected counties was in the top quartile of counties nationwide. Further, the median home value for more than one-third of the selected counties was in the top 10 percent of median home values for all counties nationwide.

**Table 3: Home Value Indicators, Source, Use, and Findings of GAO Analysis of NFIP Policies**

| Indicator | Source | Use | Finding |
|---|---|---|---|
| County median home value | 2007 through 2011 American Community Survey (ACS) 5-year data for all U.S. counties | Analyzed the data to determine relative ranking of the 351 selected counties relative to all counties. | Counties with the highest and lower home values tended to have larger percentages of remaining subsidized policies than nonsubsidized policies in Special Flood Hazard Areas (SFHA). |
| Amount of building coverage for each single-unit primary residence policy located in an SFHA | NFIP policy database | Analyzed the data to determine the number and percentage (at different coverage amounts) of remaining subsidized and nonsubsidized policies. | Remaining subsidized policies generally carried lower amounts of coverage than nonsubsidized policies in SFHAs. |
| City median home value index | Zillow for 5 selected case study counties | Analyzed the data to illustrate whether different results occurred at the city level. | Results varied by location. |

Source: GAO.

[29]For our analysis of the financial characteristics of remaining subsidized and nonsubsidized policies, we used 351 counties that represented 78 percent of all remaining subsidized policies nationwide, 77 percent of all single-unit primary residence remaining subsidized policies, and 77 percent of all NFIP policies. We selected all counties with more than 500 remaining subsidized single-unit primary residence policies and the five counties in every state (and Puerto Rico) with the most remaining subsidized policies for single-unit primary residences regardless of number.

The results of our analysis of home values varied depending on the indicator and the location. Our analysis showed that in the counties with the highest and lower median home values the percentage of remaining subsidized policies was larger than nonsubsidized policies in SFHAs. For example, about 43 percent of total NFIP policies in the selected 351 counties were in the highest decile of median home values, but about 43 percent of the remaining subsidized policies compared with about 35 percent of nonsubsidized policies were in these counties. Very few policies of any type were in counties in the lower deciles of median home value (deciles 6-10), however in these counties there were higher percentages and larger numbers of remaining subsidized policies than nonsubsidized policies (see table 4).

**Table 4: NFIP Policies in SFHAs by County Median Home Value Ranking, as of June 2012**

| Decile | Number (percentage) of selected counties | Number (percentage) of remaining subsidized policies (for single-unit primary residences) in these counties | Number (percentage) of nonsubsidized policies (for single-unit primary residences) in these counties | All NFIP policies in these counties[a] |
|---|---|---|---|---|
| 1 (high) | 123 (35.04%) | 217,329 (42.90%) | 322,923 (34.73%) | 1,814,219 (42.59%) |
| 2 | 63 (17.95%) | 131,302 (26.12%) | 453,286 (48.74%) | 1,480,097 (34.74%) |
| 3 | 46 (13.11%) | 49,477 (9.77%) | 72,220 (7.77%) | 354,644 (8.32%) |
| 4 | 44 (12.54%) | 47,875 (9.45%) | 50,626 (5.44%) | 419,550 (9.85%) |
| 5 | 33 (9.40%) | 33,565 (6.63%) | 18,947 (2.04%) | 122,106 (2.87%) |
| 6 | 19 (5.41%) | 11,177 (2.21%) | 3,905 (0.42%) | 26,801 (0.63%) |
| 7 | 13 (3.70%) | 10,988 (2.17%) | 6,742 (0.72%) | 33,056 (0.78%) |
| 8 | 5 (1.42%) | 1,499 (0.30%) | 208 (0.02%) | 2,948 (0.07%) |
| 9 | 3 (0.85%) | 1,651 (0.33%) | 816 (0.09%) | 4,591 (0.11%) |
| 10 (low) | 2 (0.57%) | 710 (0.14%) | 266 (0.03%) | 2,156 (0.05%) |
| Total | 351 | 506,572 | 929,940 | 4,260,169 |

Source: GAO analysis of FEMA and ACS data.

Note: Deciles are determined using 2007 through 2011 American Community Survey (ACS) 5-year estimates on county median home values for the 50 states, Washington, D.C., and Puerto Rico.

[a]Includes all flood zones.

Our analysis of coverage amounts found that remaining subsidized policies generally carried smaller NFIP coverage amounts than nonsubsidized policies in SFHAs, a possible indicator of lower home values.[30] As shown in figure 7, a smaller percentage of remaining subsidized policies had the maximum coverage of $250,000 than nonsubsidized policies (29 percent versus about 50 percent). Also, a larger percentage of remaining subsidized policies had less than $100,000 in building coverage than nonsubsidized policies (26 percent versus 8 percent). The results of our comparison of coverage amounts could indicate that the subsidized policies were for lower-valued properties, but the perceived flood risk and cost of coverage also could affect the coverage amount. Finally, a larger percentage of V-zone policies had the maximum coverage amount than the A-zone policies but represented a small fraction of all SFHA policies. Further details of our analysis by flood zone appear in appendix II.

---

[30]As noted earlier, FEMA does not have information on the fair market value of properties covered by flood insurance, but the agency does have information on the amount of coverage carried on a property. Coverage amount is not a perfect proxy for home value because it is limited by NFIP's maximum building coverage amount of $250,000 per residential unit. However, coverage amount can give an indication of a property's value relative to other properties.

**Figure 7: Percentage of NFIP Policies in SFHAs by Building Coverage Amounts in Selected Counties, as of June 2012**

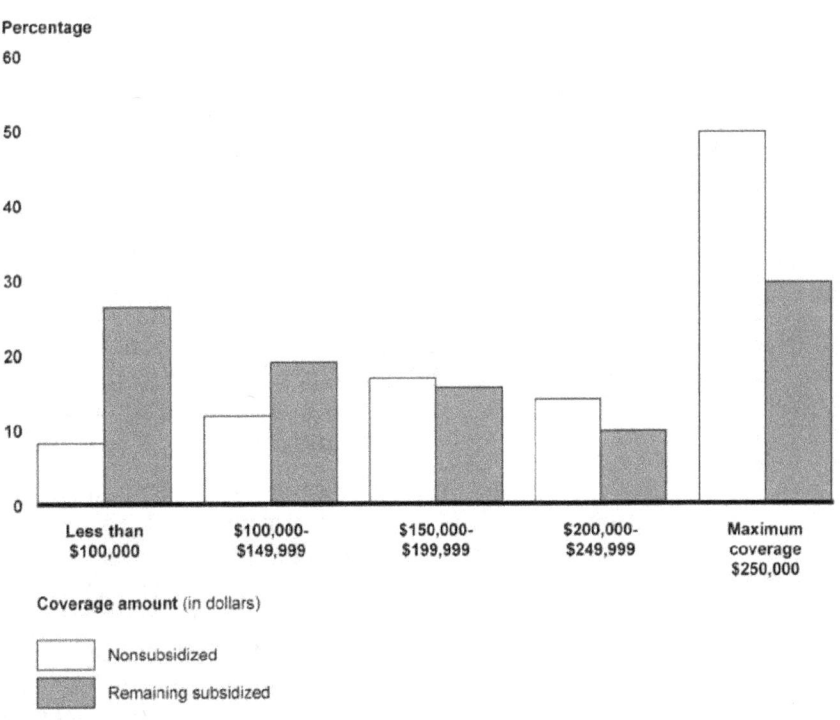

Percentage

Coverage amount (in dollars)

☐ Nonsubsidized

▨ Remaining subsidized

Source: GAO analysis of FEMA data.

Note: The selected 351 counties comprise 77 percent of total NFIP policies.

We analyzed NFIP coverage amounts (on single-unit primary residence nonsubsidized policies and remaining subsidized policies in SFHAs) and county median home values together and found that higher coverage amounts were associated with higher county median home values. Counties with higher median home values had larger percentages of both remaining subsidized policies and nonsubsidized policies at the NFIP maximum coverage level of $250,000 than counties with lower median home values. In addition, counties with lower median home values generally had larger percentages of remaining subsidized policies and nonsubsidized policies with lower amounts of coverage (less than $100,000) than counties with higher median home values. However, nonsubsidized policies consistently had higher amounts of coverage. In every decile of county median home value, a larger percentage of nonsubsidized policies had the maximum amount of NFIP coverage than remaining subsidized policies, while a smaller percentage of nonsubsidized policies had lower amounts of coverage (less than

$100,000) than remaining subsidized policies. Additional details of the combined analysis are presented in appendix II.

We performed five case studies to illustrate results in specific counties. The case studies offer a more in-depth, within county view (how characteristics vary across cities within select counties). We performed the NFIP coverage and median home value analyses, but also used publicly available real estate data to examine city-level median home values within the county.[31] These cases are illustrative only and are not nationwide indicators, and some of the results from these case studies matched our earlier results and some did not. Los Angeles County is one illustration of how NFIP policies compared within a county, but other counties had different results. The results of the other case study counties are presented in appendix II.

---

**Case Study: Los Angeles County, California**

- Los Angeles County had a median home value in the top 10 percent of all counties and consistent with our earlier results had a higher percentage of remaining subsidized policies than nonsubsidized policies in SFHAs (more than twice as many policies).
- Consistent with our analysis of NFIP coverage amounts, a lower percentage of remaining subsidized policies in Los Angeles County had maximum building coverage than nonsubsidized policies (59 versus 77 percent), but a higher percentage had building coverage less than $100,000 (6 versus 3 percent).
- However, Los Angeles County also had a high percentage of both subsidized and nonsubsidized policies with maximum NFIP coverage and a low percentage of both types of policies at lower levels of coverage.
- Our analysis of the city median home value in Los Angeles County found that about 88 percent of remaining subsidized and nonsubsidized policies were in cities in the second and third quartiles of median home value.
- Additionally, although Los Angeles County is located on the Pacific Ocean, it had 120 V-zone (high-risk velocity coastal) policies compared to about 6,000 A-zone (high-risk) policies. Ninety-seven of the V-zone policies were remaining subsidized policies and all were located in a single city with a median home value in the top quartile of median home value.

---

[31]We used Zillow city-level median home value index data from January 2013.

Income Level

Comparing policies in SFHAs in the selected counties, our analysis showed that in counties with the highest and lowest median household incomes, there were a larger percentage of remaining subsidized policies than nonsubsidized policies. We used county median household income from the 2007 through 2011 ACS 5-year data for all U.S. counties as an indicator of household income for property owners. We analyzed the data to determine relative ranking of the 351 selected counties relative to all counties and compared the number and percentage of properties that would continue to receive subsidized rates with properties charged full-risk rates. In general, most of all of the policies in our analysis were in counties with higher median household income (deciles 1-4), with fewer policies in the counties with lower median household income counties. However, counties in the highest and lowest decile in median household income had higher percentages of remaining subsidized policies than nonsubsidized policies (see table 5). For example, 19 percent of all policies in the 351 selected counties were in the highest decile of median household income. But about 29 percent of the remaining subsidized policies were in these counties versus about 11 percent of nonsubsidized policies. One percent of all policies in the selected counties were in the lowest decile of median household income. But 4 percent of the remaining subsidized policies were in these counties versus 1 percent of nonsubsidized policies.

Table 5: NFIP Policies in SFHAs by County Median Household Income Ranking, as of June 2012

| Decile | Number (percentage) of selected counties | Number (percentage) of remaining subsidized policies (for single-unit primary residences) in these counties | Number (percentage) of nonsubsidized policies (for single-unit primary residences) in these counties | All NFIP policies in these counties[a] |
|---|---|---|---|---|
| 1 (high) | 90 (25.64%) | 146,801 (28.98%) | 103,624 (11.14%) | 826,647 (19.40%) |
| 2 | 70 (19.94%) | 95,802 (18.91%) | 153,852 (16.54%) | 1,066,461 (25.03%) |
| 3 | 50 (14.25%) | 87,316 (17.24%) | 375,420 (40.37%) | 1,058,017 (24.84%) |
| 4 | 36 (10.26%) | 55,030 (10.86%) | 60,313 (6.49%) | 346,222 (8.13%) |
| 5 | 36 (10.26%) | 50,225 (9.91%) | 174,085 (18.72%) | 641,907 (15.07%) |
| 6 | 20 (5.70%) | 17,010 (3.36%) | 12,622 (1.36%) | 112,674 (2.64%) |

| Decile | Number (percentage) of selected counties | Number (percentage) of remaining subsidized policies (for single-unit primary residences) in these counties | Number (percentage) of nonsubsidized policies (for single-unit primary residences) in these counties | All NFIP policies in these counties[a] |
|---|---|---|---|---|
| 7 | 13 | 8,086 | 7,718 | 33,307 |
| | (3.70%) | (1.60%) | (0.83%) | (0.78%) |
| 8 | 13 | 22,653 | 29,103 | 118,893 |
| | (3.70%) | (4.47%) | (3.13%) | (2.79%) |
| 9 | 7 | 2,874 | 1,319 | 9,946 |
| | (1.99%) | (0.57%) | (0.14%) | (0.23%) |
| 10 (low) | 16[b] | 20,774 | 11,885 | 46,095 |
| | (4.56%) | (4.10%) | (1.28%) | (1.08%) |
| Total | 351 | 506,572 | 929,940 | 4,260,169 |

Source: GAO analysis of NFIP and ACS data.

Note: Deciles are determined using 2007 through 2011 American Community Survey (ACS) 5-year estimates on county median home values for the 50 states, Washington, D.C., and Puerto Rico.

[a]Includes all flood zones.

[b]Fourteen of the 16 counties in the tenth decile were in Puerto Rico.

We also examined home value and household income indicators together. Selected counties with the highest median household incomes and highest median home values had higher percentages of remaining subsidized policies than nonsubsidized policies in SFHAs. For example, 78 of the 351 selected counties were in the highest decile category for both median home value and median household income. About 26 percent of remaining subsidized policies were in these counties, compared with 7 percent of nonsubsidized policies. Selected counties with higher median household income generally also had higher median home values, but counties with higher median home values did not always have higher median incomes. Higher percentages of remaining subsidized policies than nonsubsidized policies were found in counties with lower median home values and lower median household incomes. More detail on these results can be found in appendix II.

## Data Constraints Limit FEMA's Ability to Estimate the Cost of Subsidies and Establish Full-Risk Rates on Previously Subsidized Policies

The cost of subsidized policies to NFIP can be measured in terms of forgone net premiums (the difference between subsidized and full-risk rates, adjusted for premium-related expenses). However, FEMA does not have the historical program data needed to make this calculation. Because of this constraint, estimating the historic cost of subsidies on NFIP is difficult. FEMA also does not have information on the flood risk of properties with previously subsidized rates, which is needed to establish full-risk rates for these properties going forward.

### Historical Cost of Subsidies Difficult to Estimate

FEMA does not have sufficient data to estimate the aggregate cost of subsidies. Since fiscal year 2002, FEMA's annual actuarial rate reviews have included an estimated range of the percentage of the full-risk premiums that policyholders with subsidized premiums pay. (We refer to this as the subsidy rate). FEMA based these estimated ranges, in part, on the analysis in a 1999 report conducted by PricewaterhouseCoopers (PwC), which sampled pre-FIRM structures around the nation and collected information on elevation of the properties to calculate what the full-risk rates on these properties would have been.[32] FEMA has continued to use this report as the basis for estimating the percentage of the full-risk rate that subsidized policyholders pay.[33] Since fiscal year 2002, NFIP has reported that the estimated subsidized premium rate is

---

[32]PricewaterhouseCoopers, *FEMA: Study of the Economic Effects of Charging Actuarially Based Premium Rates for Pre-FIRM Structures* (May 14, 1999).

[33]According to FEMA, subsidized premium rates are based on full-risk rates, and full-risk rates are based on the probability of a given level of flooding, damage estimates based on that level of flooding, and accepted actuarial principles. To determine subsidized premium rates, FEMA subtracts the total amount that it expects to collect on full-risk rate premiums from the average historical loss year target, which is the minimum amount of premium the program needs to collect to cover at least average annual losses, as determined by historical loss data. The amount remaining from this calculation is the aggregate target amount of subsidized premiums that the program needs to collect. To set individual subsidized rates, FEMA officials then consider their knowledge of flood risks, previous rate increases for various areas, and statutory limits on increases. Beginning in 2007, FEMA instituted a discounted weight for catastrophic loss years; however the Biggert-Waters Act requires that these years now be included in the calculation of the average loss year.

between 35 and 45 percent of the full-risk premium rate.[34] FEMA officials said that they did not report an estimate before the 1999 PwC report. Therefore, determining forgone premiums without these estimates would be difficult because the percentage of subsidized premium rates compared with full-risk rates may have varied considerably over time.

Although it was not possible to estimate forgone premiums since the program was established, the following provides information about the impact of subsidized premiums on the program.

- Data are not available from FEMA to estimate the forgone premiums before 2002. Using FEMA's estimated range of subsidy rates to actual premiums collected from 2002 through 2011, we conducted an analysis to estimate the premiums that could have been collected if subsidies had not existed over that period.[35] FEMA officials have clarified their estimate that 2011 subsidized premiums represented 40 percent to 45 percent of full-risk premium rates, explaining that after paying for all administrative and other expenses, the remaining premiums would cover about 40 to 45 percent of the expected average long-term annual losses.
- Premiums are used to cover not only claims, but also operating expenses and any debt. According to FEMA officials, 17 percent of forgone premiums would be needed to pay operating expenses that would increase if subsidized premiums were increased. Such expenses consist of premium taxes (about 2 to 2.5 percent of premium) and agents' commissions associated with the private insurance companies that sell and service NFIP policies (about 15 percent of premium). Therefore, about 83 percent would be available to help cover fixed expenses (which do not vary with premiums) and

---

[34]In its actuarial rate review for 2011, FEMA estimated that currently subsidized policy rates were between 40 and 45 percent of full-risk premium rates. See FEMA, *National Flood Insurance Program: Actuarial Rate Review* (Washington, D.C.: October 2011). Prior ranges were between 35 and 40 percent. According to FEMA officials, FEMA changed the estimated range of the percentage of full-risk premiums that subsidized policyholders pay from 35 to 40 percent to 40 to 45 percent, after gradual increases in this percentage over the last several years. However, in commenting on a draft of this report, FEMA officials informed us that this percentage was actually the portion of subsidized premiums available to pay expected average long-term annual losses.

[35]In comments on a draft of this report FEMA officials provided new information about variable expenses that could impact this estimate. GAO plans to undertake additional work to analyze the impact of these variables on our initial estimate of the financial impact of subsidized premiums on the program and report the results separately.

to pay losses. During years when losses are less than average, the program potentially generates a surplus. During higher-loss years, accumulated surplus could be used to help pay the insured flood losses that exceed that year's net premium revenue and reduce the likelihood of needing to borrow from Treasury. Therefore, additional premiums could have helped offset FEMA's need to borrow or put the agency in a better position to manage catastrophic losses or repay its debt.

- A similar number but higher percentage of policies were subsidized in the earlier years of the program, therefore, most of the program's premium revenue did not reflect the risk of flooding. In 1978 about 76 percent of policies were subsidized compared with about 20 percent in 2012. The Flood Disaster Protection Act of 1973 expanded the use of premium subsidies to encourage the purchase of flood insurance and introduced mandatory flood insurance purchase requirements in SFHAs as a condition of receipt of direct federal and federally related financial assistance related to the property. For the next 7 years, the subsidized premiums remained in effect. During this period, nearly every community with a flood hazard joined NFIP, and policies in force reached 2 million by 1979.

- The percentage of full-risk premiums that policyholders with subsidized rates paid was also lower than today. When the program began, NFIP administrators set the subsidized rates on the basis of what they considered affordable.[36] However, from 1981 through 1986, FEMA initiated a series of rate increases for all subsidized policies. The increases were intended to generate premiums at least sufficient to cover expenses and losses relative to the historical average loss year when combined with the premiums paid by policyholders with full-risk rates. Since 1986, additional rate increases have been made to bring the average program premium to a level intended to be sufficient to pay for the historical average loss year and have additional funds available to service its debt to Treasury.

## Mandated Information on Claims and Premiums Associated with Subsidized Policies

As mandated in the Biggert-Waters Act, we also calculated the claims and premiums attributable to all policies that received subsidies (historically subsidized policies) since 1978 and to policies with characteristics similar to remaining subsidized policies (remaining subsidized policies). While the difference between claims and premiums is not a meaningful measure of the costs of subsidies because premiums

---

[36]GAO-09-12.

are used to pay not only claims but other costs of administering the program, they provide additional descriptive information. Moreover, because flooding is a highly variable event, with losses varying widely from year to year, even analysis of the decades of historical data available could lead to unreliable conclusions about actual flood risks. Based on our analysis of NFIP claims data, we calculated the amount of claims attributable to historically subsidized policies from 1978 through 2011 to have been $24.1 billion, of which $15.2 billion is attributable to remaining subsidized policies. NFIP had $28.5 billion in claims for policies charged at the full-risk premium rates in the same time period. Based on data provided by FEMA on all subsidized premiums, we calculated the amount of premiums collected for all historically subsidized policies from 1978 through 2011 to have been $26.2 billion, of which $15.7 billion is attributable to remaining subsidized policies. Comparatively, FEMA collected $33.7 billion in premiums for policies with full-risk premium rates for the same time period.

## FEMA Lacks the Information Needed to Establish Full-Risk Rates That Reflect Risk of Flooding for Remaining Subsidized Policies

FEMA generally lacks information to establish full-risk rates that reflect flood risk for active policies that no longer qualify for subsidies as a result of the Biggert-Waters Act and also lacks a plan for proactively obtaining such information.[37] The act requires FEMA to phase in full-risk rates on these policies. Federal internal control standards state that agencies should identify and analyze risks associated with achieving program objectives, and use this information as a basis for developing a plan for mitigating the risks. In addition, these standards state that agencies should identify and obtain relevant and needed data to be able to meet program goals.

FEMA does not have key information used in determining full-risk rates from all policyholders. According to FEMA officials, not all policyholders have elevation certificates, which document their property's risk of flooding.[38] Information about elevation is critical for determining the location of a property in relation to the risk of flooding and is a key element in establishing premium rates. For instance, FEMA uses

---

[37]Pub. L. No. 112-141, §100205 (a)(1).

[38]Surveyors calculate the elevation of the first-level of a structure in relation to the expected flood level, or base flood elevation. According to FEMA, obtaining such a certificate typically would cost a policyholder from $500 to $2,000 or more.

elevation as one of the factors in its model to set full-risk rates for buildings constructed after the publication of a community's FIRM.[39] FEMA officials said that although a variety of factors, such as occupancy status and number of floors, are used to determine these rates, the elevation of the building is the most important factor. FEMA also uses elevation certificates as administrative tools.[40] Elevation certificates are required for some properties, but optional for others. For example, communities participating in NFIP must obtain the elevation information for all new and substantially improved structures.[41] In addition, FEMA requires elevation certificates to determine rates for post-FIRM buildings located in high-risk areas, the A and V zones. However, an elevation certificate generally has not been required for pre-FIRM buildings that previously received subsidized rates because information about elevation was not used in setting subsidized rates.[42] According to NFIP data, property elevations relative to the base flood elevation are unknown for 97 percent of both the 1.15 million historically subsidized policies and the more than 700,000 remaining subsidized policies in SFHAs.[43] As of October 2013, FEMA is requiring applicants for new policies on pre-FIRM properties that previously received subsidized rates and property owners whose coverage has lapsed to provide elevation certificates.

---

[39]This method of estimating flood damage is based on the hydrologic model, which is a static or dynamic representation of the process that affects surface water runoff. Hydrologic models are used to describe present conditions or predict future behavior of the hydrologic regime at a specific area of land that "caches" and "releases" surface water runoff (referred to as catchment). Examples of hydrologic model inputs are precipitation and snow melt and examples of outputs are stream discharge and evapotranspiration. NFIP's use of the hydrologic model to estimate loss exposure in flood-prone areas also incorporates other relevant factors, such as the building's location, construction, and elevation relative to expected flood levels.

[40]FEMA also uses the elevation certificate to document elevation information necessary to ensure compliance with community floodplain management regulations and to support requests for revisions of FIRMs.

[41]Under NFIP, communities are required to obtain the elevation of the lowest floor (including basement) of all new and substantially improved structures and maintain a record of all such information [44 C.F.R. § 60.3(b)(5)].

[42]An elevation certificate may be required if the pre-FIRM building is being rated under the optional post-FIRM flood insurance rules. About half of the older pre-FIRM buildings insured by NFIP have documented their compliance with new construction standards and pay full-risk rates.

[43]More than 99 percent of the remaining subsidized policies are located in SFHAs.

FEMA is phasing-in rate increases for other policyholders who no longer qualify for subsidies and is relying on policyholders to voluntarily provide elevation certificates. With the 1999 PwC report as a basis for an estimate of the full-risk rate for subsidized policies, FEMA officials said they have been using the assumption that subsidized rates are about half of the full-risk rates and have begun implementing premium increases of at least 100 percent for all active policies that are having their subsidies eliminated. According to FEMA, they will phase in these increases at 25 percent per year, consistent with the act, for several years until the rates reach a specific level or until policyholders supply an elevation certificate that indicates the property's risk, allowing FEMA to determine the full-risk rate. If policyholders voluntarily obtain an elevation certificate that shows that their risk is lower, they may be able to qualify for lower rates or it may not take as many years of rate increases to reach the full-risk rate. However, policyholders at higher risks could be subject to even higher rates. According to FEMA officials, it will take several years for previously subsidized policies to reach a full-risk rate and the agency will communicate to policyholders to encourage them to purchase elevation certificates to determine their actual flood risk. For example, FEMA has posted information on its website about program changes as a result of the Biggert-Waters Act and the importance of obtaining elevation certificates.

Although subsidized policies have been identified as a risk to the program because of the financial drain they represent, FEMA does not have a plan to expeditiously and proactively obtain the information needed to set full-risk rates for all of them. Instead, FEMA will rely on certain policyholders to voluntarily obtain elevation certificates. Those at lower risk levels have an incentive to do so because they can qualify for lower rates. However, policyholders with higher risk levels have a disincentive to voluntarily obtain an elevation certificate because they could end up paying an even higher premium. Without a plan to expeditiously obtain property-level elevation information, FEMA will continue to lack basic information needed to accurately determine flood risk and will continue to base full-risk rate increases for previously subsidized policies on limited estimates. As a result, FEMA's phased-in rates for previously subsidized policies still may not reflect a property's full risk of flooding, with some policyholders paying premiums that are below and others paying premiums that exceed full-risk rates. As we have previously found, not accurately identifying the actual risk of flooding increases the likelihood that premiums may not be adequate and adds to concerns about NFIP's financial stability.[44]

## Several Options Exist for Reducing the Financial Impact of Remaining Subsidized Policies

Through our previous work as well as interviews we conducted and literature we reviewed for this report, we identified three broad options that could help address NFIP's financial situation: (1) adjust the pace of the elimination of subsidies, (2) target assistance or remaining subsidies by the financial need of property owners, and (3) increase mitigation efforts. In prior work, we discussed similar options for addressing the impact of subsidized policies and the work we conducted for this report confirmed that, with some modifications to reflect the changes from the Biggert-Waters Act, these were still generally the prevailing options.[45] In addition, our previous and current work have shown that each of the options has advantages and disadvantages in terms of the impact on the program's public policy goals and would involve trade-offs that would have to be weighed. For example, charging premium rates that fully reflect the risk of flooding could help improve the financial condition of NFIP and limit taxpayer costs before and after a disaster. However, eliminating or reducing subsidized policies could have unintended consequences, such as increasing premium rates to the point that flood insurance is no longer affordable for some policyholders and potential declines in program participation.

### Adjust the Pace of the Elimination of Subsidies

Accelerating the elimination of subsidies could improve NFIP's financial stability by more quickly increasing the number of policies that more accurately reflect the risk of flooding.[46] NFIP would be able to charge more policyholders premium rates that more closely reflect the losses that FEMA expected to incur, contributing to the financial health of NFIP. Insurance industry representatives and floodplain managers we interviewed noted that they supported reducing the number of subsidized policies and moving to full-risk rates. For example, a representative of an insurance industry association said that the provisions in the Biggert-Waters Act for the elimination of subsidies and rate increases are only a partial step and that implementing these provisions would help people better understand their risk of flooding and related costs for the area

---

[44]See GAO, *High-Risk Series: An Update,* GAO-13-283 (Washington, D.C.: Feb. 2013).

[45]GAO-09-20.

[46]GAO-09-20.

where they lived. Stakeholders also noted that the threat of increased premium rates would encourage some policyholders affected by Superstorm Sandy to undertake mitigation efforts as they repaired their properties.

Although accelerating the elimination of subsidies could strengthen the financial solvency of the program, it also entails trade-offs and unintended consequences. For example, according to FEMA estimates, the elimination of subsidies for pre-FIRM properties would on average more than double these policyholders' premium rates, raising concerns about the affordability of the coverage and participation in the program. Higher premium rates might result in reduced participation in NFIP over time as people either decide to drop their policies or are priced out of the market, according to FEMA officials and insurance industry stakeholders we interviewed. The 1999 PwC study estimated that, for communities most likely to experience a decrease in property values if subsidies were immediately eliminated, on average 50 percent of policyholders might cancel their coverage. It is too soon to tell the long-term impacts of the elimination of subsidies that went into effect in 2013. Even reducing, rather than eliminating, subsidies could increase the financial burden on some existing policyholders—particularly low-income policyholders—and could lead to some of them deciding to leave the program. As a result, if owners of pre-FIRM properties, which have relatively high flood losses, cancelled their insurance policies, the federal government—and ultimately taxpayers—could face increased costs in the form of FEMA disaster assistance grants to these individuals.[47] However, according to a recent study, a large proportion of disaster assistance is provided to states, versus directly to individuals, and the assistance provided to individuals via grants and low-interest loans is fairly limited in size.[48] An additional trade-off associated with making immediate increases to premium rates is resistance from local communities. Stakeholders we interviewed further noted that increased insurance costs might make some properties more difficult to sell, particularly pre-FIRM properties in older, inland communities at high risk of flooding.

---

[47]Owners of properties located in SFHAs must participate in NFIP to be eligible to receive federal assistance following a presidentially declared disaster event.

[48]See Erwann Michel-Kerjan, "*Have We Entered an Ever-Growing Cycle on Government Disaster Relief?*" The Wharton School, University of Pennsylvania (Mar. 15, 2013).

Delaying the elimination of subsidized policies could address stakeholder concerns about the affordability of flood insurance and the time frames in the Biggert-Waters Act for implementing full-risk rates, but also has trade-offs. For example, while stakeholders we interviewed supported provisions of the act to reduce the number of subsidized policies and moving to full-risk rates, they said that the time frames in the act were aggressive and could be burdensome for low-income policyholders. They also stated that more gradual increases for certain policyholders could keep policies more affordable. They noted there have been proposals to delay the elimination of subsidies and phasing in of full-risk rates. However, delaying the elimination of subsidies would continue to expose the federal government to increased financial risk. And, as previously noted, not charging full-risk rates contributes to FEMA's ongoing management challenges in maintaining the financial stability of NFIP. NFIP has been on our high-risk list since 2006 because of concerns about its long-term financial solvency and management issues.[49] While Congress and FEMA intended that, insofar as practicable, NFIP be funded with premiums collected from policyholders, the program was, by design, not actuarially sound.

## Target Assistance or Remaining Subsidies Based on Financial Need of Property Owner

Targeting assistance, based on financial need, could help ensure that only those in need receive subsidies, with the rest paying full-risk rates. This assistance could take several forms, including direct assistance through NFIP, tax credits, grants, or vouchers. For example, other federal programs have targeted subsidies through means tests or other methods. Such an approach could help ensure that those needing the subsidy would have access to it and retain their coverage. Alternatively, stakeholders we interviewed for this report noted that FEMA could replace the subsidies with vouchers based on financial need to offset higher premiums. For example, the Department of Housing and Urban Development's Housing Choice Voucher program is administered by public housing agencies that collect information on applicants' income and assets to determine eligibility and voucher amounts.[50] Similar data on flood insurance policyholders could be collected to assess need, determine eligibility, and provide appropriate amounts of financial assistance to families that otherwise could not afford their flood insurance premiums.

---

[49]GAO-13-359T.

[50]24 C.F.R. Part 982.

According to industry stakeholders we interviewed, targeting assistance based on financial need would help make the planned phased-in premium increases more affordable. In a recent paper on flood insurance affordability, the Association of State Floodplain Managers (ASFPM) suggested that a flood insurance voucher program could be developed for low-income policyholders who may not be able to afford the rate increases or for those who might need time to adjust to premium increases.[51] ASFPM's paper also noted that, while the premium rate increases required by the Biggert-Waters Act will improve the financial stability of NFIP, those increases could have a significant impact on flood insurance affordability for low-income policyholders. In particular, the ASFPM paper states that assistance will be necessary for some policyholders to help them transition to either full-risk rates, or to mitigate their properties, otherwise some property owners might not be able to afford to remain in their homes. Other insurance industry representatives and stakeholders have also cited affordability concerns and suggested that as full-risk rates were phased in, assistance for low-income individuals could be provided through a voucher system or program based on financial need. A provision of the act requires FEMA to study NFIP participation and affordability issues, including offering vouchers based on income.[52] According to FEMA officials, as of May 31, 2013, FEMA has consulted with the National Academy of Sciences about determining how to undertake this study.

As previously discussed, our comparison of characteristics (such as median income and median home values) associated with remaining subsidized and nonsubsidized policies indicates that applying full-risk rates may be overly burdensome for some property owners and not for others. For example, we found a higher percentage of subsidized policies in both counties with lower and very high incomes, indicating that in certain areas, some subsidized policyholders may find higher flood insurance rates difficult to afford, while those who were located in higher-income areas may be able to afford premium increases.

However, it could be challenging for FEMA to develop and administer such an assistance program in the midst of ongoing management

---

[51]See Association of State Floodplain Mangers, Inc., "*Flood Insurance Affordability*" (Madison, Wis.: Apr. 26, 2013).

[52]Pub. L. No. 112-141, §100236.

challenges. Specifically, we have previously found that FEMA has faced significant management challenges in areas that affect NFIP, including strategic and human capital planning; collaboration among offices; and record, financial, and acquisition management.[53] In addition, in previous work we found that FEMA has faced challenges modernizing NFIP's insurance policy and claims management system. Implementing a financial assistance program would require FEMA to plan and develop new processes. Representatives from a national insurance professional organization we interviewed for this report stated that it would be difficult for FEMA to administer an assistance program and ensure that an evaluation for assistance was done consistently. In addition, they said that to administer an assistance program such as vouchers, tax credits, or grants through the Write-Your-Own companies (insurance companies that sell and service flood insurance for NFIP), a process would be needed to ensure that means-testing is evaluated and administered consistently. They also suggested that it would be easier to administer a program if all policyholders were charged a full-risk rate, with a separate process that would allow them to apply for assistance, based on financial need.

## Increase Mitigation Efforts

A third option to address the financial impact of subsidized premium rates on NFIP would be to substantially expand mitigation efforts to ensure that more homes were better protected from flooding, including making mitigation mandatory. Mitigation efforts such as elevation, relocation, and demolition can be used to help reduce or eliminate the long-term risk of flood damage to structures insured by NFIP. However, mitigation of pre-FIRM properties is voluntary unless a property has been substantially damaged or the owner undertook substantial improvement.[54]

We previously reported that mitigation efforts could be targeted to properties that have been most costly to the program, such as those with "repetitive losses."[55] In addition, we noted in our prior work that this would have the advantage of producing savings for policyholders and for federal taxpayers through reduced flood insurance losses and federal disaster

---

[53]GAO-11-297.

[54]If the cost of restoring a flood-damaged structure to its predamage condition or renovating an insured structure is equal to or greater than 50 percent of that structure's market value before the damage or renovation, the structure must be mitigated and meet other applicable local ordinance requirements. See 44 C.F.R. §59.1 and 60.3(c)(2).

[55]GAO-09-20.

assistance. While the Biggert-Waters Act eliminated subsidies for severe repetitive loss properties and for prospective policyholders who refuse to accept any offer for mitigation assistance (including an offer to relocate) following a major disaster, properties not built to meet a community's flood resistant requirements or in the highest-risk zones could face more severe damages in the event of a flood.[56] Insurance industry stakeholders agreed that mitigation could be used to reduce future financial risk for NFIP.

Stakeholders we spoke to for this report also commented that since such mitigation measures often are done at the community level, offering community-based policies could help encourage more mitigation. This is consistent with our prior work in which local officials generally support increased mitigation efforts.[57] Industry stakeholders also commented that incorporating community-based flood insurance into NFIP could help leverage community resources for mitigation projects that would benefit the entire community, rather than individual structures. For example, floodplain mangers noted that with a community-based policy, the local unit of government could assess fees on all properties benefitting from community mitigation measures. In addition, because the premium rate would be on a community versus structure basis, the community, not the property owner, generally would make development or neighborhood-type decisions that either increased or decreased risk in the community.

Disadvantages associated with mitigation as an option to reduce the financial impact of the subsidized policies include the expense to NFIP, taxpayers, and communities. For example, implementing mitigation measures for tens of thousands of properties that continue to receive subsidized rates could take a number of years to complete, which could have an on-going risk to NFIP's financial health. We have previously reported that increasing mitigation would be costly and require increased funding. Furthermore, we found in our past and current work that buyouts and relocations would be more costly in certain areas of the country and in some cases the cost for mitigating older structures might be prohibitive. The effectiveness of mitigation efforts could be limited by FEMA's reliance on local communities with varying resources. For example, not all

---

[56]Pub. L. No. 112-141, §100205, classified as amended at 42 U.S.C. 4014(g)(3) and (4).

[57]GAO-09-20.

communities have the staff or resources to fully carry out mitigation, meet cost-sharing requirements, and enforce compliance.

As we reported in 2008, even when federal funds are made available to a community and property owners are interested in mitigating their properties, property owners still may have to pay a portion of the mitigation expenses, which could discourage participation in mitigation efforts.[58] In interviews for this report, stakeholders said that mitigation was expensive and that as premiums are increased to full-risk rates, some means of assistance would be helpful for policyholders who may have difficulty paying for mitigation efforts. Mitigation costs would have to be weighed against mitigation benefits (possible savings from a decrease in flood damage).

In addition, certain types of mitigation, such as relocation or demolition, might be met with resistance by communities that rely on those properties for tax revenues, such as coastal communities with significant development in areas prone to flooding. Furthermore, mitigation activities are often constrained by conflicting local interests, cost concerns, and a lack of public awareness of the risks of natural hazards and the importance of mitigation. Communities' economic interests often can conflict with long-term hazard mitigation goals. For example, a community with a goal of economic growth might allow development to occur in hazard-prone areas (along the coast or in floodplains).

Our analysis indicates that the three options discussed above are not mutually exclusive and may be used together to reduce the financial impact of subsidized policies on NFIP. For example, accelerating the elimination of subsidies could be done in conjunction with targeting assistance to only those policyholders who need help to retain their flood insurance—thus advancing the goal of strengthening the financial solvency of NFIP and addressing affordability concerns for low-income policyholders. In addition, FEMA may be able to build on its existing mitigation efforts and target assistance for mitigation efforts to those policyholders who need financial assistance. The way in which an option is implemented, such as more aggressively or gradually, also can produce different effects in terms of policy goals and thus change the advantages and disadvantages (see table 6).

---

[58] GAO-09-20.

**Table 6: Advantages and Disadvantages of Options for Reducing the Financial Impact of Remaining Subsidized Premium Rate Policies**

| Option | Advantages | Disadvantages |
|---|---|---|
| Adjust the pace of reducing or eliminating subsidies | • Accelerating the pace of reducing or eliminating subsidies would more quickly charge more property owners premium rates that more accurately reflect the risk of flood loss (decrease the inventory of subsidized properties)<br><br>• Higher premium rates could motivate property owners to undertake mitigation to reduce their rates<br><br>• Would provide more accurate information to homeowners about their risk of flooding | • Accelerating the pace of reducing or eliminating subsidies could reduce program participation, both at the policyholder and community levels, potentially resulting in increased costs to taxpayers of providing disaster assistance for catastrophic events<br><br>• Could be resisted by local communities because of potential negative impact on residents and local economy<br><br>• Many policyholders of subsidized properties do not have elevation certificates to determine their risk level. |
| Base subsidies on the financial need of policyholder | • Would charge more property owners premium rates that more accurately reflect the risk of flood loss (decrease the inventory of subsidized properties)<br><br>• Would continue to benefit those in greatest financial need by keeping rates affordable<br><br>• Higher premium rates for some could motivate property owners to undertake mitigation to reduce their rates | • Increased premium rates for some could reduce program participation<br><br>• Requiring property owners to apply for subsidies could reduce participation for those in greatest need<br><br>• Implementing a new program in the midst of existing management and oversight challenges could pose additional challenges for FEMA and the insurance companies that sell and service flood insurance. |
| Increase mitigation efforts | • Could reduce flood losses, especially by focusing mitigation efforts on properties with repetitive losses<br><br>• Could increase the number of property owners paying full-risk rates by denying subsidized rates to those who refuse mitigation offers<br><br>• Could receive support from local communities because of potential positive effect of mitigation on property values | • Extensive mitigation efforts could be expensive for taxpayers<br><br>• Extensive mitigation efforts could take years to complete and subsidized rates would continue to negatively affect NFIP's financial health in the interim<br><br>• Effectiveness of mitigation efforts could be limited by heavy reliance on local communities with varying resources |

Sources: GAO, insurance experts, FEMA, and other stakeholders.

# Conclusions

While FEMA has taken initial steps to eliminate subsidies for various types of properties in accordance with the Biggert-Waters Act requirements, eliminating the more than 700,000 additional policies that continue to receive subsidies will take many years to accomplish. Subsidies on some policies will be eliminated as properties are sold or if coverage lapses, but FEMA has some data limitations and implementation issues to resolve before other subsidies identified in the act can be eliminated. With some efforts under way, FEMA has much work ahead of it in planning and executing implementation of the changes in the act as well as effectively managing NFIP.

Although FEMA has information on premiums and claims paid for subsidized policies over time, it does not have the information needed to determine the appropriate premium amounts policyholders should pay to reflect the full level of risk for floods. To phase out and eventually eliminate subsidies and revise rates over time, FEMA will need information on the relative risk of flooding and property elevations (elevation certificates), which generally had not been required for subsidized policies prior to the Biggert-Waters Act. The act requires FEMA to phase in full-risk rates on policies that previously received subsidies. According to federal internal control standards, agencies should identify and analyze risks associated with achieving program objectives, and use this information as a basis for developing a plan for mitigating the risks and obtaining needed information. Going forward, FEMA will require new policyholders and those whose coverage has lapsed to provide elevation information when renewing or obtaining new policies; however, FEMA will rely on other policyholders who previously received subsidized rates to voluntarily provide this information. As FEMA continues to implement the requirements of the act to charge full-risk rates, the agency plans to assume that all subsidized policies pay about half of the full-risk premium and has begun phasing-in rate increases based on this factor for all active policies that are having their subsidies removed. Without a plan to require all policyholders to obtain elevation certificates to accurately document their property elevations and relative risk of flooding, FEMA will lack information that is key to determining appropriate full-risk rate premiums. As a result, the rates that FEMA plans to implement may not adequately reflect a property's actual flood risk, and some policyholders may be charged too much and some too little for their premiums.

## Recommendation for Executive Action

To establish full-risk rates for properties with previously subsidized rates that reflect their risk for flooding, we recommend that the Secretary of the Department of Homeland Security (DHS) direct the FEMA Administrator to develop and implement a plan, including a timeline, to obtain needed elevation information as soon as practicable.

## Agency Comments and Our Evaluation

We provided a draft of this report to DHS for its review and comment. DHS provided written comments that are presented in appendix III. The letter noted that the department concurred with our recommendation to develop and implement a plan to obtain elevation information from previously subsidized policyholders. The letter stated that FEMA will evaluate the appropriate approach for obtaining or requiring the submittal of this information. In particular, the letter noted that although obtaining this information cost-effectively presents significant challenges, FEMA will explore technological advancements and engage with industry to determine the availability of technology, building information data, readily available elevation data, and current flood hazard data that could be used to implement the recommendation. FEMA also provided technical comments, which we have incorporated into the report, as appropriate.

We are sending copies of this report to the appropriate congressional committees and the Secretary of Homeland Security. In addition, the report is available at no charge on the GAO website at http://www.gao.gov.

If you have any questions about this report, please contact me at (202) 512-8678 or cackleya@gao.gov. Contact points for our Offices of Congressional Relations and Public Affairs may be found on the last page of this report. GAO staff who made key contributions to this report are listed in appendix IV.

Alicia Puente Cackley
Director, Financial Markets
and Community Investment

# Appendix I: Objectives, Scope, and Methodology

The Biggert-Waters Flood Insurance Reform Act of 2012 (Biggert-Waters Act) mandated that GAO conduct a number of studies, including this study on the properties that continue to receive subsidized rates after the implementation of the act and options to further reduce these subsidies.[1] This report discusses (1) the number, location, and financial characteristics of properties that continue to receive subsidized rates compared with full-risk rate properties, (2) information needed to estimate the historic financial impact of subsidies and establish rates that reflect the risk of flooding on properties with previously subsidized rates, and (3) options to reduce the financial impact of remaining subsidized properties.

Although the Biggert-Waters Act mandated that GAO report on certain characteristics of the remaining subsidized policies and properties, the National Flood Insurance Program (NFIP) databases do not contain information to address several elements listed in the act. Therefore, to the extent possible, we developed alternative methodologies to address the elements of the act.

## Number, Location, and Financial Characteristics of Properties That Continue to Receive Subsidized Rates Compared with Full-Risk Rate Properties

To provide information on the number and location of NFIP-insured properties that would continue to receive subsidized premium rates, we analyzed data from NFIP's policy and repetitive loss databases as of June 30, 2012. We applied the Federal Emergency Management Agency's (FEMA) algorithm to determine which policies were subsidized, and applied FEMA's interpretation of the provisions in the Biggert-Waters Act that eliminate subsidies to determine which policies would retain their subsidies.[2] We also analyzed NFIP's legislative history and relied on FEMA's implementation of legislative requirements authorizing subsidized rates for certain properties in high-risk locations.

To determine the fair market value of properties that would continue to receive subsidized premium rates, we used other NFIP data and publicly available information as indicators of value because the fair market values required by the act were not available in NFIP's databases. We used three indicators of home value, (1) NFIP policy-level coverage

---

[1]Pub. L. No. 112-141, §100231.

[2]We used the NFIP data as of June 30, 2012, as it was the current data at the passage of the Biggert-Waters Act. To determine primary residence, we used NFIP principal residence field. We included all nonresidential policies as business policies.

amounts, (2) 2007 through 2011 5-year American Community Survey
(ACS) county-level data on median home values, and (3) January 2013,
Zillow city-level median home value index within case study counties.[3]
For consistency in our message, we compared all the indicators at the
county-level. To place NFIP policies in counties, we used ZIP code
information contained in the NFIP policy file as of June 30, 2012, and
matched those data with U.S. Postal Service and Department of Housing
and Urban Development ZIP code to county data (as of December 2011).
For ZIP codes that crossed county borders, we assigned policies
proportionally to the counties based on the fields available in the ZIP code
to county file.

We aggregated the total number of policies and remaining subsidized
policies for all counties, and selected 351 counties for our analysis that
contained the majority of the policies. We selected all counties with 500 or
more remaining subsidized policies for single-unit, primary residences
(247 counties). We also included the five counties in each state and
Puerto Rico with the most remaining subsidized policies for single-unit
primary residences, regardless of the total number in the county, to better
ensure a comprehensive national representation. Accordingly, the 351
counties we selected represent 78 percent of all remaining subsidized
policies nationwide, 77 percent of all remaining subsidized policies for
single-unit primary residences, and 77 percent of all NFIP policies. As
more than 99 percent of remaining subsidized policies were in Special
Flood Hazard Areas (SFHA), we limited our comparison with
nonsubsidized policies to those for single-unit primary residences in
SFHAs.

We used NFIP policy data as of June 30, 2012, on coverage amounts as
the first indicator of home value. To determine how building coverage
amounts compared between remaining subsidized and nonsubsidized
policies, we categorized NFIP building coverage amounts using less than
$100,000, $100,000-$149,999, $150,000-$199,999, $200,000-$249,999,
and $250,000, which is the maximum coverage for residential units. We
compared the percentage of policies of each type within each category of
coverage at the county level for the selected counties. We also conducted

---

[3]The American Community Survey is a nationwide continuous survey conducted by the
U.S. Census Bureau. The estimates are based on multiyear period estimates for 2007
through 2011 and should not be interpreted as estimates for any particular year in the
period. Zillow is a real estate website that includes estimated market values for houses.

this analysis using flood zones, comparing the coverage amounts for A-
zone and V-zone policies separately. (The A and V flood zones represent
areas at high risk for flooding, and V zones also indicate coastal areas.)
Coverage amount as an indicator for home value is limited because NFIP
has a maximum building coverage amount of $250,000 per residential
unit. Additionally, the perceived flood risk and cost of coverage could
affect the coverage amount. However, coverage amount can give an
indication of a property's value relative to other properties.

As a second indicator of home value, we used 2007 through 2011 ACS 5-
year county-level estimates for median home values (known as B25077)
for all counties in the United States and also included the District of
Columbia and Puerto Rico. We included Puerto Rico because of its
relatively large number of NFIP policies. We used 5-year data because
other ACS data sets did not contain data for all the 351 selected counties.
Using county median home value, we ranked all counties and determined
the deciles for the 351 selected counties. We compared the percentage of
remaining subsidized with nonsubsidized policies from the selected
counties in each decile. Because these data are at the county level, areas
within the county of relatively high or low home values are
indistinguishable. We also analyzed the ACS and NFIP coverage data
together, at the county level.

As a third indicator of home value, we used Zillow city-level median home
value data as of January 2013, within five selected counties. For the
purposes of our county case study analysis, we selected the Zillow Home
Value Index because it was publicly available; covered more housing
units at the city level than other housing indices; was estimated at a
smaller geographic region; and only included nonforeclosure housing
units. We judgmentally selected five case study counties and compared
data at the city level within the county to provide more detailed
illustrations of how home values for properties that continue to receive
subsidies compare with those that pay full-risk rates. These cases are not
projectable to all counties. We selected our case study counties based on
the number of relevant NFIP policies, their location, and the reliability of
the data for the county. Specifically, we selected counties with at least
1,000 remaining subsidized policies and nonsubsidized policies for single-
unit primary residences. We selected one county from each of the four
states with the most remaining subsidized policies. We selected Pinellas
County, Florida; Los Angeles County, California; and Ocean County, New
Jersey; however, the Zillow data for Louisiana did not meet our level of
reliability and was eliminated. As Pinellas County is on the Gulf of Mexico,
Los Angeles County is on the Pacific Ocean, and Ocean County is on the

Atlantic Ocean, we chose the other two counties to represent inland
flooding—Cook County, Illinois, and Pima County, Arizona. The Zillow
information for these counties met our criteria for data reliability. For each
county, we determined which NFIP policies may be located in the county
based on ZIP code. Because the NFIP city name was not consistently
entered, two analysts independently matched the NFIP policy city names
to Zillow city names within the county. A third analyst served as the
mediator for differences using alternative location information. Within
each county, we ranked the cities by median home value and distributed
them into quartiles. We compared the number and percentage of
remaining subsidized policies with the nonsubsidized policies in the cities
in each quartile. Additionally, for each case study county, we reviewed the
results from the NFIP coverage and ACS analyses within the county.

Because owner income data were not available in NFIP's databases, we
analyzed 2007 through 2011 ACS 5-year data as an indicator of income
levels of owners of remaining subsidized properties.[4] We used 5-year,
county-level data on median household incomes (B19013) for all counties
in the United States, the District of Columbia, and Puerto Rico. Using the
median household income data, we ranked all counties and determined
the deciles for the 351 selected counties. We compared the percentage of
remaining subsidized policies with nonsubsidized policies in SFHAs from
the selected counties in each decile. Because these data are at the
county level, areas within the county of relatively high or low household
incomes are indistinguishable. We also analyzed the ACS median home
value and median household income data together, at the county level.

Because consistent, nationwide aggregate data on sales prices for each
property covered by a remaining subsidized pre-Flood Insurance Rate
Map (FIRM) policy since 1968 were not available from NFIP or other
sources, we determined that the home value analysis was sufficiently
similar to provide an indication of sales prices to respond to this study
element.

We also used NFIP policy fiscal year-end data from 2002 through 2012 to
estimate the potential annual rate of decline in the number of remaining
subsidized policies over time. Consistent, nationwide aggregate data on
sales dates for each pre-FIRM property since 1968 were not available

---

[4]We were unable to determine additional indicators of income level.

from NFIP or other sources. We compared sequential years of policy data
to determine whether each policy with the characteristics of a remaining
subsidized policy continued to have coverage. We first matched company
and policy data and if no match was found, matched on owner name.[5] If a
policy in the first year failed to match by either method, we assumed that
the policy no longer had coverage. We estimated the annual rate of
decline for 10 sequential year pairs. We compared our results with a
recent NFIP policy tenure study by calculating the decline rate from the
reported tenure rate. We estimated the number of remaining subsidized
policies over a 30-year period given the different annual decline rates.

Because data were not available from NFIP on the number of times each
pre-FIRM property had been sold, we determined that the policy decline
rate analysis was sufficiently similar to provide an indication of extent of
ownership or length of time policies remained in the program to respond
to this study element.

Additionally, because data were not available from NFIP's databases on
the extent to which pre-FIRM properties are currently owned by the same
owners as at the time of the original NFIP rate map, we determined that
the policy decline rate analysis was sufficiently similar to provide an
indication of extent of ownership or length of time policies remained in the
program to respond to this study element.

## Estimated Historic Financial Impact of Subsidized Properties on NFIP

To estimate the financial impact, or cost, of subsidized properties to NFIP,
we attempted to calculate forgone premiums—lost revenue to the
program in premiums—due to subsidies. Because data on elevations of
NFIP subsidized properties were not available to determine the total
forgone premiums from subsidized policies, we used FEMA's estimates of
the subsidy rate from 2002 through 2011 to estimate a range of forgone
premiums attributable to subsidized properties in this period. We limited
our analysis to 2002 through 2011 because FEMA did not estimate
subsidy rates prior to 2002. Lacking the information to calculate the
ranges associated with the premiums that would have been collected, we
made assumptions based on limited historical information from FEMA,
including the annual Actuarial Rate Reviews from 2002 through 2011,

---

[5]We performed the match on last name except when data were missing in the last name
field. In these cases, we performed the match on the first name.

which state that subsidized premiums were estimated to be between 35
and 45 percent of the full-risk premium (the subsidy rate). Our analysis
did not adjust for potential effects on behavior (such as on program
participation) or changes in operating expenses that could have occurred
had historical rates not been subsidized. In addition, our analysis did not
account for new information provided by FEMA officials that only a portion
of subsidized premiums is available to pay for losses. We plan to analyze
the impact of this new information provided by FEMA in comments on a
draft of this report. We will report the methodology and results of our
estimate separately. FEMA did not report such estimates from 1978
through 2001.

For the period before 2002, we analyzed a prior GAO report, FEMA's
annual actuarial review, and a PricewaterhouseCoopers study
commissioned by FEMA and present qualitative information about the
cost of subsidies. Additionally, because of the limited historical program
data from FEMA, developing a sufficiently reliable year-by-year or state-
by-state estimate of cost to NFIP as a result of remaining subsidized
policies is not possible.

To estimate the total losses incurred by subsidized properties since the
establishment of NFIP and compare these with the total losses incurred
by all structures charged a nonsubsidized premium rate, we analyzed
NFIP claims database as of June 30, 2012, to determine total losses
attributable to remaining subsidized and nonsubsidized policies. Data
were not available before 2002 that would allow us to determine whether
a policy had the characteristics of a remaining subsidized policy. For
years prior to 2002, we estimated the proportion of claims for previously
subsidized policies that were attributable to remaining subsidized policies,
based on the average proportion in the claims data in the latest 10 years.

To determine the premium income collected by NFIP as a result of
subsidized policies, compared with premium income collected from
properties charged a nonsubsidized rate, we analyzed annual NFIP
premium data and data broken out by subsidy to determine the annual
premiums of remaining subsidized and nonsubsidized policies. We
estimated the proportion of previously subsidized premiums attributable to
remaining subsidized policies based on the average proportion in the
latest 10 years of NFIP policy data.

## Options to Reduce the Financial Impact of Remaining Subsidized Properties

To determine the options to reduce the financial impact of remaining properties with subsidized policies, we analyzed NFIP's legislative history and reviewed FEMA documents as well as documents from insurance industry organizations and academic institutions to gather information on options to eliminate or reduce the financial impact of subsidized policies on NFIP. In addition, we interviewed NFIP officials and representatives of insurance industry organizations and floodplain managers. We also interviewed a nationally recognized academic knowledgeable about the financial impact and the public policy challenges associated with catastrophic events, and discussed previous studies on NFIP and other relevant studies on flood insurance issues.

For all data sets used we performed data testing and gathered information from issuing entities about possible data limitations. For the ACS, Zillow, and NFIP data sets, we interviewed officials on usability and reliability. We determined that each data set used was sufficiently reliable for our intended purposes.

We conducted this performance audit from September 2012 to July 2013 in accordance with generally accepted government auditing standards. Those standards require that we plan and perform the audit to obtain sufficient, appropriate evidence to provide a reasonable basis for our findings and conclusions based on our audit objectives. We believe that the evidence obtained provides a reasonable basis for our findings and conclusions based on our audit objectives.

# Appendix II: Comparison of Remaining Subsidized Policies with Nonsubsidized Policies in Special Flood Hazard Areas

We compared various characteristics of the remaining subsidized policies and nonsubsidized policies in SFHAs in selected counties. In addition, we conducted more detailed analysis of five counties for illustrative purposes.

## Selected Counties

For our analysis of the financial characteristics of subsidized and nonsubsidized policies in SFHAs, we selected 351 counties that represented 78 percent of all remaining subsidized policies nationwide, 77 percent of all remaining subsidized policies for single-unit primary residences, and 77 percent of all NFIP policies. We selected all counties with more than 500 remaining subsidized policies for single-unit primary residences and the five counties in every state (and Puerto Rico) with the most remaining subsidized policies, regardless of number. Figure 8 shows the 351 selected counties and the number of remaining subsidized policies for single-unit primary residences under NFIP.

**Figure 8: Top Five Counties per State and Counties with 500 or More Remaining Subsidized Policies for Single-Unit Primary Residences, as of June 2012**

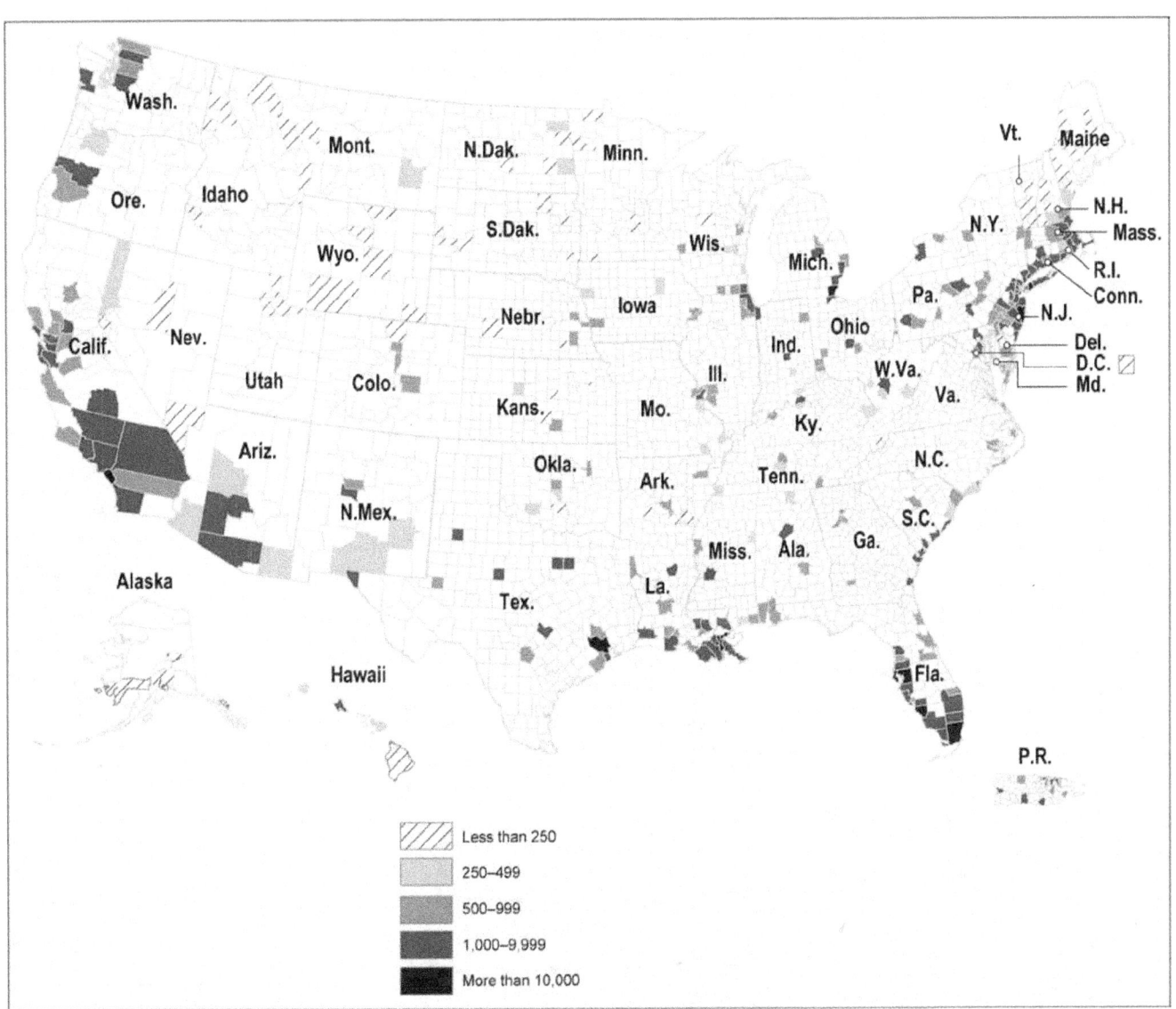

Sources: GAO analysis of FEMA data; Map Resources (map).

## Analysis of Coverage Amounts by Flood Zone

For both remaining subsidized policies and nonsubsidized policies, a larger percentage of policies in V zones (coastal areas with a high risk of flooding) had the maximum coverage amount than policies in A zones (noncoastal areas with a high risk of flooding) (see fig. 9).[1] Also for both types of policies, V-zone policies represented a very small fraction of all policies in SFHAs. For example, 1.6 percent of remaining subsidized policies and 0.8 percent of nonsubsidized policies in SFHAs were in V zones.

**Figure 9: Percentage of NFIP Policies for Single-Unit Primary Residences, by Flood Zone in 351 Selected Counties, as of June 2012**

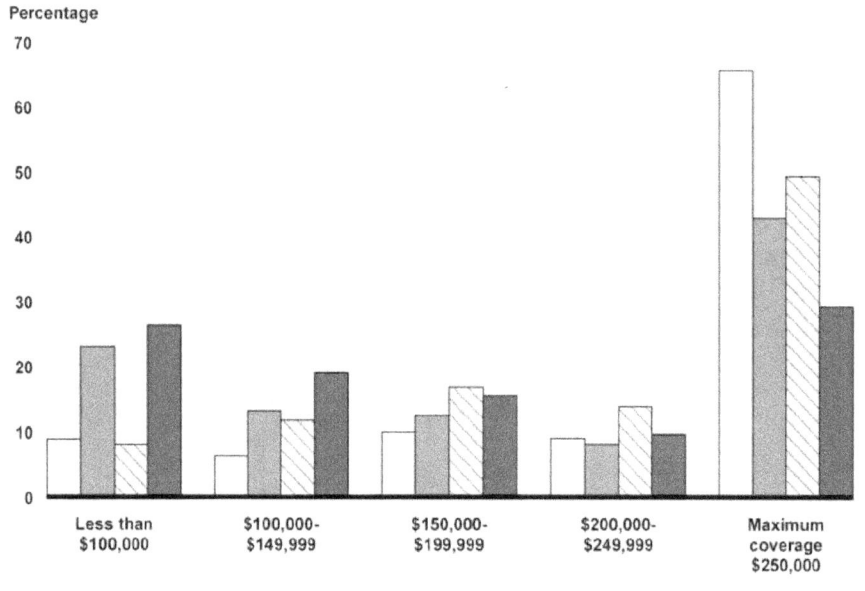

Percentage

Coverage amount (in dollars)

Nonsubsidized V-zone N=7,406

Remaining subsidized V-zone N=8,029

Nonsubsidized A-zone N=922,534

Remaining subsidized A-zone N=498,543

Source: GAO analysis of FEMA data.

Note: N represents the number of policies in the category.

[1] A and V flood zone areas comprise the SFHAs.

## Combined County Median Home Value and NFIP Coverage Amount Analysis

We analyzed NFIP coverage amounts (for remaining subsidized policies and nonsubsidized policies in SFHAs for single-unit primary residences) and county median home values together and determined that higher coverage amounts were associated with higher county median home values. Counties with higher median home values had higher percentages of remaining subsidized policies and nonsubsidized policies with the NFIP maximum coverage of $250,000 than counties with lower median home values (see table 7). In addition, counties with lower median home values generally had higher percentages of remaining subsidized policies and nonsubsidized policies with lower amounts of coverage (less than $100,000) than counties with higher median home values. However, nonsubsidized policies consistently had higher amounts of coverage. Specifically, in every decile of county median home value, a larger percentage of nonsubsidized policies had the maximum amount of NFIP coverage than remaining subsidized policies. Also in every decile of county median home value, a smaller percentage of nonsubsidized policies had lower amounts of coverage (less than $100,000) than remaining subsidized policies.

**Table 7: Percentage of NFIP Policies in SFHAs by Building Coverage Amount (Dollars) and County Median Home Value Ranking for Nonsubsidized and Subsidized Policies, as of June 2012**

| Decile | Nonsubsidized policies | | | | | Remaining subsidized policies | | | | |
|---|---|---|---|---|---|---|---|---|---|---|
| | Less than $100,000 | $100,000 -149,999 | $150,000 -249,999 | $200,000 -249,999 | Maximum coverage $250,000 | Less than $100,000 | $100,000 -149,999 | $150,000 -249,999 | $200,000 -249,999 | Maximum coverage $250,000 |
| 1 (high) | 5.83% | 8.97% | 14.73% | 12.91% | 57.56% | 11.67% | 11.25% | 14.67% | 12.39% | 50.03% |
| 2 | 5.94 | 10.70 | 17.47 | 15.25 | 50.65 | 22.94 | 23.01 | 19.75 | 10.87 | 23.44 |
| 3 | 13.39 | 19.05 | 20.18 | 13.68 | 33.70 | 37.44 | 29.67 | 17.41 | 7.04 | 8.44 |
| 4 | 16.67 | 21.50 | 19.30 | 11.09 | 31.44 | 46.36 | 27.95 | 13.47 | 5.01 | 7.22 |
| 5 | 28.79 | 21.92 | 18.28 | 10.23 | 20.79 | 54.52 | 25.34 | 11.48 | 4.06 | 4.59 |
| 6 | 51.24 | 22.91 | 12.36 | 5.45 | 8.05 | 68.16 | 19.66 | 7.31 | 2.54 | 2.33 |
| 7 | 49.58 | 24.13 | 12.95 | 5.97 | 7.36 | 75.66 | 16.00 | 5.64 | 1.48 | 1.22 |
| 8 | 47.24 | 20.10 | 12.17 | 7.61 | 12.87 | 70.23 | 21.70 | 6.28 | 0.80 | 1.00 |
| 9 | 41.16 | 20.89 | 17.15 | 8.59 | 12.21 | 70.16 | 17.41 | 7.32 | 2.18 | 2.93 |
| 10 (low) | 45.68 | 20.44 | 15.06 | 6.13 | 12.70 | 68.33 | 18.06 | 7.93 | 3.38 | 2.31 |

Source: GAO analysis of FEMA and ACS data.

Note: This analysis uses 2007 through 2011 American Community Survey (ACS) 5-year data on median home value.

## Combined County Median Home Value and Median Household Income Analysis

We analyzed home value and household income indicators together and found that counties with the highest median household incomes and highest median home values had higher percentages of remaining subsidized policies than nonsubsidized policies in SFHAs. For example, 78 of the 351 selected counties were in the highest decile in both median home value and median household income (see table 8).

**Table 8: Selected Counties by Median Home Value and Median Household Income Deciles, as of June 2010**

| | | County median home value | | | | | | | | | | |
|---|---|---|---|---|---|---|---|---|---|---|---|---|
| | Decile | 1 | 2 | 3 | 4 | 5 | 6 | 7 | 8 | 9 | 10 | Total |
| County median household income | 1 | 78 | 7 | 4 | | 1 | | | | | | 90 |
| | 2 | 31 | 18 | 11 | 10 | | | | | | | 70 |
| | 3 | 7 | 14 | 10 | 10 | 7 | 1 | | 1 | | | 50 |
| | 4 | 2 | 12 | 6 | 7 | 4 | 3 | 1 | | | 1 | 36 |
| | 5 | 2 | 6 | 6 | 7 | 7 | 5 | 2 | 1 | | | 36 |
| | 6 | 2 | 2 | 5 | 3 | 3 | 1 | 3 | | 1 | | 20 |
| | 7 | | 2 | 1 | | 5 | 1 | 2 | 2 | | | 13 |
| | 8 | | 1 | | 5 | 3 | 1 | 2 | 1 | | | 13 |
| | 9 | 1 | | | | | 4 | 1 | | | 1 | 7 |
| | 10 | | 1 | 3 | 2 | 3 | 3 | 2 | | 2 | | 16 |
| | Total | 123 | 63 | 46 | 44 | 33 | 19 | 13 | 5 | 3 | 2 | 351 |

Source: GAO analysis of ACS and FEMA data.

Note: This analysis uses 2007 through 2011 American Community Survey (ACS) 5-year data on median home value and median household income.

About 26 percent of remaining subsidized policies compared with 7 percent of nonsubsidized policies in SFHAs were in these counties (see table 9). Remaining subsidized policies were also found in higher percentages than nonsubsidized policies in counties with lower median income and lower median household counties (lowest 6 deciles). Counties with higher median household income generally also had higher median home values, but counties with higher median home values did not always have higher median incomes.

Table 9: NFIP Policies in SFHAs in Selected Counties by Median Home Value and Median Household Income Deciles

| | | | | | | County median home value | | | | | | |
|---|---|---|---|---|---|---|---|---|---|---|---|---|
| decile | 1 (high) | 2 | 3 | 4 | 5 | 6 | 7 | 8 | 9 | 10 (low) | Total |
| **1 (high)** | Remaining Subsidized Policies | | | | | | | | | | | |
| | 133,968 (26.45%) | 6,504 (1.28%) | 6,220 (1.23%) | | 109 (0.02%) | | | | | | 146,801 (28.98%) |
| | Nonsubsidized Policies | | | | | | | | | | | |
| | 68,174 (7.33%) | 16,929 (1.82%) | 18,497 (1.99%) | | 24 (0.00%) | | | | | | 103,624 (11.14%) |
| **2** | Remaining Subsidized Policies | | | | | | | | | | | |
| | 56,164 (11.09%) | 10,119 (2.00%) | 8,476 (1.67%) | 21,043 (4.15%) | | | | | | | 95,802 (18.91%) |
| | Nonsubsidized Policies | | | | | | | | | | | |
| | 101,728 (10.94%) | 10,534 (1.13%) | 8,866 (0.95%) | 32,723 (3.52%) | | | | | | | 153,852 (16.54%) |
| **3** | Remaining Subsidized Policies | | | | | | | | | | | |
| | 9,422 (1.86%) | 54,171 (10.69%) | 5,153 (1.02%) | 8,921 (1.76%) | 8,703 (1.72%) | 228 (0.04%) | | 717 (0.14%) | | | 87,316 (17.24%) |
| | Nonsubsidized Policies | | | | | | | | | | | |
| | 29,515 (3.17%) | 333,755 (35.89%) | 5,043 (0.54%) | 4,356 (0.47%) | 2,602 (0.28%) | 103 (0.01%) | | 46 (0.00%) | | | 375,420 (40.37%) |
| **4** | Remaining Subsidized Policies | | | | | | | | | | | |
| | 282 (0.06%) | 35,716 (7.05%) | 9,636 (1.90%) | 5,530 (1.09%) | 2,137 (0.42%) | 1,005 (0.20%) | 298 (0.06%) | | | 427 (0.08%) | 55,030 (10.86%) |
| | Nonsubsidized Policies | | | | | | | | | | | |
| | 65 (0.01%) | 43,608 (4.69%) | 10,631 (1.14%) | 4,983 (0.54%) | 655 (0.07%) | 319 (0.03%) | 5 (0.00%) | | | 39 (0.00%) | 60,313 (6.49%) |
| **5** | Remaining Subsidized Policies | | | | | | | | | | | |
| | 14,982 (2.96%) | 5,269 (1.04%) | 11,322 (2.23%) | 4,029 (0.80%) | 7,946 (1.57%) | 4,681 (0.92%) | 1,806 (0.36%) | 190 (0.04%) | | | 50,225 (9.91%) |
| | Nonsubsidized Policies | | | | | | | | | | | |
| | 121,921 (13.11%) | 20,197 (2.17%) | 23,620 (2.54%) | 1,058 (0.11%) | 4,529 (0.49%) | 724 (0.08%) | 2,032 (0.22%) | 3 (0.00%) | | | 174,085 (18.72%) |

| County median household income | decile | | 1 (high) | 2 | 3 | 4 | 5 | 6 | 7 | 8 | 9 | 10 (low) | Total |
|---|---|---|---|---|---|---|---|---|---|---|---|---|---|
| | 6 | Remaining Subsidized Policies | | | | | | | | | | | |
| | | | 1,694 (0.33%) | 1,054 (0.21%) | 3,255 (0.64%) | 2,654 (0.52%) | 4,257 (0.84%) | 314 (0.06%) | 3,464 (0.68%) | | 318 (0.06%) | | 17,010 (3.36%) |
| | | Nonsubsidized Policies | | | | | | | | | | | |
| | | | 1,324 (0.14%) | 3,277 (0.35%) | 2,012 (0.22%) | 3,304 (0.36%) | 1,948 (0.21%) | 12 (0.00%) | 655 (0.07%) | | 89 (0.01%) | | 12,622 (1.36%) |
| | 7 | Remaining Subsidized Policies | | | | | | | | | | | |
| | | | | 596 (0.12%) | 127 (0.03%) | | 5,329 (1.05%) | 523 (0.10%) | 1,160 (0.23%) | 351 (0.07%) | | | 8,086 (1.60%) |
| | | Nonsubsidized Policies | | | | | | | | | | | |
| | | | | 688 (0.07%) | 23 (0.00%) | | 5,183 (0.56%) | 46 (0.00%) | 1,679 (0.18%) | 99 (0.01%) | | | 7,718 (0.83%) |
| | 8 | Remaining Subsidized Policies | | | | | | | | | | | |
| | | | | 15,510 (3.06%) | | 2,943 (0.58%) | 2,637 (0.52%) | 451 (0.09%) | 871 (0.17%) | 241 (0.05%) | | | 22,653 (4.47%) |
| | | Nonsubsidized Policies | | | | | | | | | | | |
| | | | | 22,874 (2.46%) | | 2,372 (0.26%) | 2,233 (0.24%) | 389 (0.04%) | 1,174 (0.13%) | 60 (0.01%) | | | 29,103 (3.13%) |
| | 9 | Remaining Subsidized Policies | | | | | | | | | | | |
| | | | 817 (0.16%) | | | | | 1,401 (0.28%) | 372 (0.07%) | | | 284 (0.06%) | 2,874 (0.57%) |
| | | Nonsubsidized Policies | | | | | | | | | | | |
| | | | 195 (0.02%) | | | | | 682 (0.07%) | 214 (0.02%) | | | 227 (0.02%) | 1,319 (0.14%) |
| | 10 (low) | Remaining Subsidized Policies | | | | | | | | | | | |
| | | | | 3,362 (0.66%) | 5,288 (1.04%) | 2,754 (0.54%) | 2,447 (0.48%) | 2,573 (0.51%) | 3,016 (0.60%) | | 1,333 (0.26%) | | 20,774 (4.10%) |
| | | Nonsubsidized Policies | | | | | | | | | | | |
| | | | | 1,424 (0.15%) | 3,528 (0.38%) | 1,829 (0.20%) | 1,764 (0.19%) | 1,629 (0.18%) | 983 (0.11%) | | 727 (0.08%) | | 11,885 (1.28%) |

County median home value

| | | | | | County median home value | | | | | | |
|---|---|---|---|---|---|---|---|---|---|---|---|
| decile | 1 (high) | 2 | 3 | 4 | 5 | 6 | 7 | 8 | 9 | 10 (low) | Total |
| | **Remaining Subsidized Policies** | | | | | | | | | | |
| Total | 217,329 (42.90%) | 132,302 (26.12%) | 49,477 (9.77%) | 47,875 (9.45%) | 33,565 (6.63%) | 11,177 (2.21%) | 10,988 (2.17%) | 1,499 (0.30%) | 1,651 (0.33%) | 710 (0.14%) | 506,572 (100.00%) |
| | **Nonsubsidized Policies** | | | | | | | | | | |
| | 322,923 (34.73%) | 453,286 (48.74%) | 72,220 (7.77%) | 50,626 (5.44%) | 18,947 (2.04%) | 3,905 (0.42%) | 6,742 (0.72%) | 208 (0.02%) | 816 (0.09%) | 266 (0.03%) | 929,940 (100.00%) |

Source: GAO analysis of ACS and FEMA data.

Note: This analysis uses 2007 through 2011 American Community Survey (ACS) 5-year estimates on median home value and median household income.

## Case Study Counties

We performed five case studies to illustrate results in specific counties (see fig. 10).[2] We selected the counties based on the number of relevant NFIP policies, location, and reliability of city-level data.[3] Case studies were chosen to offer a more in-depth, within county view (how things vary across cities within select counties). We performed the NFIP coverage and median home value analyses, but also used publicly available real estate data to examine city-level median home values within the county.[4] We compared remaining subsidized and nonsubsidized policies in SFHAs (A and V flood zones are designated as SFHAs).These cases cannot be projected nationwide, and the results of our analysis from each county are independent of each other. Some of the results from these case studies matched our earlier results, and some did not.

[2]We planned to perform a sixth case study in Louisiana but the Zillow data did not meet our data reliability threshold.

[3]Appendix I more fully describes our selection criteria.

[4]We used Zillow city-level median home value index data from January 2013.

**Figure 10: Case Study Counties**

| County | Number of cities and home value indicator | Policies in the analysis: | | NFIP coverage amounts SFHA | City median home value quartiles |
|---|---|---|---|---|---|

NFIP coverage amounts SFHA
- ▦ Remaining subsidized
- ▢ Nonsubsidized

Pinellas, Florida — Gulf of Mexico — Pinellas

32  ACS decile: 2

| | Remaining subsidized | Nonsubsidized |
|---|---|---|
| All | 24,149 | 19,904 |
| A-zone | 23,678 | 19,497 |
| V-zone | 471 | 407 |

Remaining subsidized pie: 17%, 9%, 15%, 59%
Nonsubsidized pie: 13%, 22%, 26%, 39%

Ocean, New Jersey — Atlantic Ocean — Ocean

46  ACS decile: 1

| | Remaining subsidized | Nonsubsidized |
|---|---|---|
| All | 10,057 | 13,052 |
| A-zone | 9,883 | 12,930 |
| V-zone | 174 | 122 |

Remaining subsidized pie: 13%, 37%, 16%, 34%
Nonsubsidized pie: 8%, 31%, 14%, 47%

Cook, Illinois — Cook

125  ACS decile: 1

| | Remaining subsidized | Nonsubsidized |
|---|---|---|
| All | 6,500 | 339 |
| A-zone | 6,500 | 339 |
| V-zone | none | none |

Remaining subsidized pie: 6%, 11%, 21%, 21%, 32%, 31%
Nonsubsidized pie: 12%, 21%, 13%, 36%, 18%

Los Angeles, California — Pacific Ocean — Los Angeles

117  ACS decile: 1

| | Remaining subsidized | Nonsubsidized |
|---|---|---|
| All | 4,298 | 1,750 |
| A-zone | 4,201 | 1,727 |
| V-zone | 97 | 23 |

Remaining subsidized pie: 4%, 7%, 45%, 43%
Nonsubsidized pie: 6%, 6%, 27%, 61%

Pima, Arizona — Pima

24  ACS decile: 2

| | Remaining subsidized | Nonsubsidized |
|---|---|---|
| All | 1,292 | 994 |
| A-zone | 1,292 | 994 |
| V-zone | none | none |

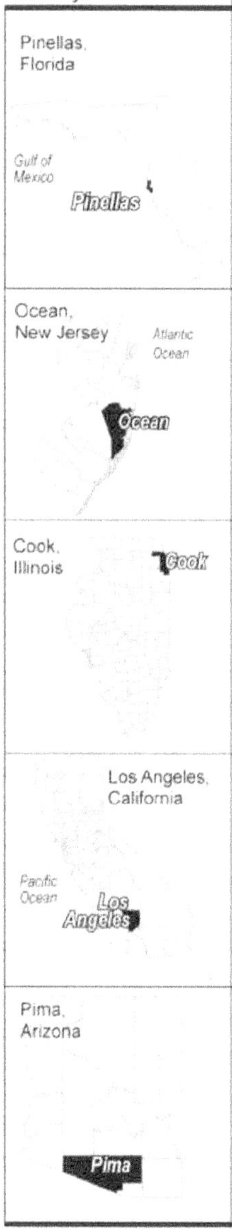

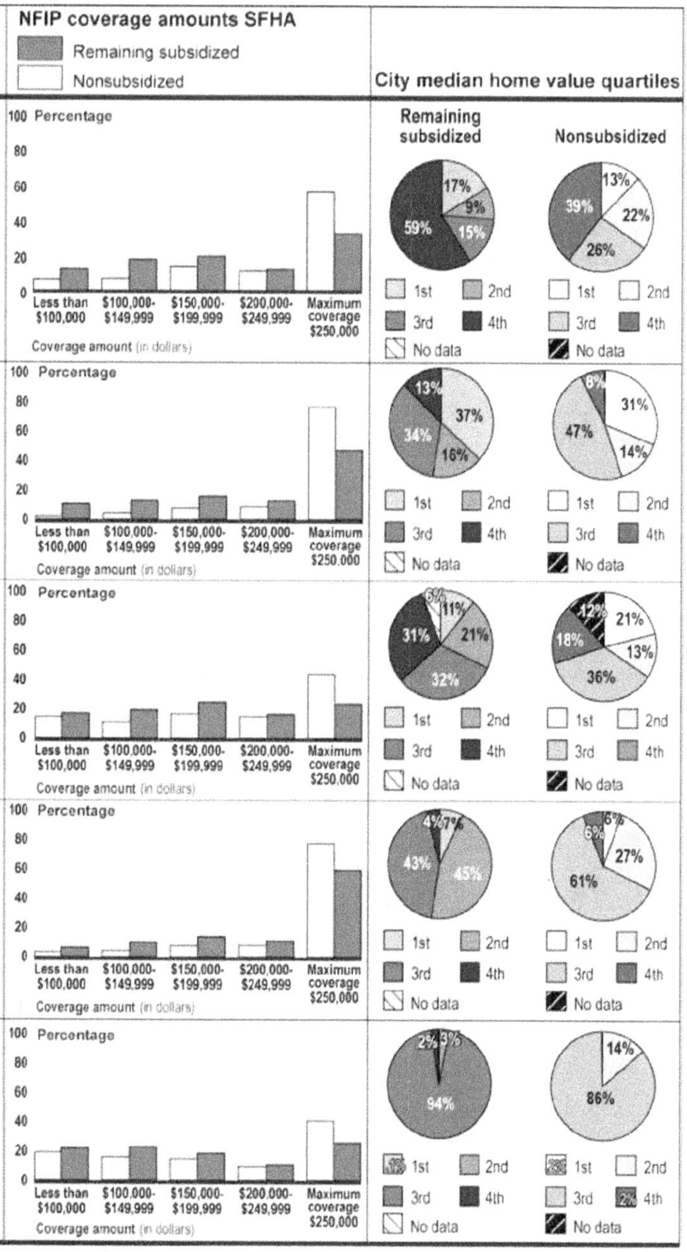

Remaining subsidized pie: 2%, 3%, 94%
Nonsubsidized pie: 14%, 86%

Legend: 1st, 2nd, 3rd, 4th, No data

Sources: GAO analysis of ACS, Zillow, and FEMA data

Note: This analysis uses 2007 through 2011 American Community Survey (ACS) 5-year data on median home value, NFIP policy data as of June 30, 2012, and Zillow city-level median home value index data as of January, 2013.

Los Angeles County, California; Ocean County, New Jersey; and Cook County, Illinois; had median home values in the top 10 percent of all counties. Consistent with our earlier results for counties with the highest median home values, Cook and Los Angeles Counties had more remaining subsidized policies than nonsubsidized policies (95 percent and 71 percent of all policies for Cook County and Los Angeles County, respectively); however, Ocean County had fewer remaining subsidized policies (about 44 percent). Los Angeles and Ocean Counties had high percentages of both subsidized and nonsubsidized policies with maximum NFIP coverage and a low percentage of both types of policies at lower levels of coverage. However, Cook County had low percentages of maximum coverage policies.

Pinellas County, Florida, and Pima County, Arizona had median home values in the second decile of all counties. Although Pinellas County had many more policies than Pima County, both had slightly more remaining subsidized policies than nonsubsidized policies (55 percent and 57 percent of all policies for Pinellas County and Pima County, respectively). Pinellas County had lower percentages of policies at maximum coverage than Los Angeles and Ocean Counties but higher percentages than Pima and Cook Counties.

Consistent with our analysis of NFIP coverage amounts, all five counties had lower percentages of remaining subsidized policies at maximum building coverage than nonsubsidized policies. Ocean County had the largest difference between nonsubsidized policies and remaining subsidized policies (77 percent versus 47 percent), and Pima County had the smallest difference (41 percent versus 26 percent). All counties had a higher percentage of remaining subsidized policies than nonsubsidized policies with building coverage less than $100,000, but in some counties the differences were smaller.

The results of our analysis of the city median home value were mixed. In all counties except Los Angeles County, higher percentages of remaining subsidized policies than nonsubsidized policies were in cities in the lowest quartile of median home value, but in Cook and Pinellas Counties the differences were larger. In Pinellas County 59 percent of the remaining subsidized policies were in cities in the lowest quartile of median home value. In the counties with V-zone policies (Los Angeles,

Ocean, and Pinellas) a slightly higher percentage of remaining subsidized policies were in cities in the highest quartile of median home value than nonsubsidized policies. In Ocean County more than 30 percent of remaining subsidized and nonsubsidized policies were in cities in the highest quartile, while in Pima County, very few policies of either type were in cities in this quartile. In Los Angeles and Pima counties, most policies of either type were in cities in the second and third quartiles. In Cook County policies were not concentrated in any quartile.

Additionally, fewer than 2 percent of policies were in V zones. Specifically, in the three counties with V-zone policies (Los Angeles, Ocean, and Pinellas) there were about 1,290 V-zone policies compared with about 72,000 A-zone policies. In each county, more V-zone policies were remaining subsidized policies than nonsubsidized policies. In Ocean and Los Angeles Counties, most V-zone policies of either type were in cities with median home values in the top quartile within the county. In Pinellas County the V-zone policies were located in cities in all quartiles of median home value.

# Appendix III: Comments from the Department of Homeland Security

U.S. Department of Homeland Security
Washington, DC 20528

Homeland
Security

June 28, 2013

Alicia Puente Cackley
Director, Financial Markets and Community Investment
U.S. Government Accountability Office
441 G Street, NW
Washington, DC 20548

Re: Draft Report GAO-13-607, "FLOOD INSURANCE: More Information Needed on
    Subsidized Properties"

Dear Ms. Cackley:

Thank you for the opportunity to review and comment on this draft report. The U.S. Department
of Homeland Security appreciates the U.S. Government Accountability Office's (GAO's) work
in planning and conducting its review and issuing this report.

The Department is pleased to note GAO's recognition of initial steps the Federal Emergency
Management Agency (FEMA) has taken to eliminate subsidies for various types of properties, in
accordance with the Biggert-Waters Flood Insurance Reform Act of 2012. Flooding is the
Nation's most common national disaster and FEMA understands that the National Flood
Insurance Program (NFIP) may be the only source of insurance against flood damage for many
residents in flood-prone areas. FEMA is committed to ensuring that NFIP delivers, as fully as
possible, on its mission of providing a means for homeowners, renters, and business owners to
financially protect themselves from floods associated with hurricanes, tropical storms, heavy
rains, and other conditions that impact the United States.

The draft report contained one recommendation with which the Department concurs.
Specifically, GAO recommended that the Secretary of Homeland Security direct the FEMA
Administrator to:

**Recommendation:** Develop and implement a plan, including a timeline, to obtain needed
elevation information and start collecting this information as soon as practicable.

**Response:** Concur. FEMA's Federal Insurance and Mitigation Administration will evaluate
approaches and estimate costs for obtaining elevation information needed to determine the full-
risk rate for policyholders.

FEMA understands the critical need for elevation information, both for the purpose of
determining the full-risk rate for policyholders, but also—and perhaps more importantly—to
provide homeowners with a true understanding of their risk. Although FEMA agrees there is
considerable merit in obtaining this type of information, FEMA is also keenly aware of the

significant challenges in obtaining this information in a cost-effective manner and with adequate precision to determine the full-risk rates for flood insurance policyholders.

While the current method for acquiring elevation information may be expensive, new and evolving methodologies and technologies may provide opportunities for FEMA to more cost effectively and otherwise obtain this information. FEMA will explore technological advancements and engage with industry to determine if this is feasible and practical. Challenges that FEMA will work through as it explores implementing this recommendation include the availability of technology, building information data, readily available elevation data, and current flood hazard data.

More specifically, FEMA will evaluate the appropriate approach, including the legal parameters, for obtaining or requiring the submittal of such data, the required level of specificity needed for accurate rate-setting of structures that do not currently have elevation data, the technical feasibility of data collection and associated costs, and recommendations for who should bear the cost of obtaining that data. Estimated Completion Date: June 30, 2014.

Again, thank you for the opportunity to review and comment on the draft report. Technical comments addressing, among other issues, GAO's estimate of the financial impact–the differences between subsidized and full-risk premium rates–to NFIP, were previously provided under separate cover. Please feel free to contact me if you have any questions. We look forward to working with you in the future.

Sincerely,

Jim H. Crumpacker
Director
Departmental GAO-OIG Liaison Office

2

# Appendix IV: GAO Contact and Staff Acknowledgments

| | |
|---|---|
| **GAO Contact** | Alicia Puente Cackley, (202) 512-8678 or cackleya@gao.gov |
| **Staff Acknowledgments** | In addition to the contact named above, Jill Naamane and Patrick Ward (Assistant Directors); William Chatlos; Barb El Osta; Christopher Forys; Isidro Gomez; Cathy Hurley; Jacquelyn Hamilton; Karen Jarzynka-Hernandez; Courtney LaFountain; May Lee; Barbara Roesmann; Jena Sinkfield; Melvin Thomas; Frank Todisco; Sonya Vartivarian; and Monique Williams made key contributions to this report. |

| | |
|---|---|
| **GAO's Mission** | The Government Accountability Office, the audit, evaluation, and investigative arm of Congress, exists to support Congress in meeting its constitutional responsibilities and to help improve the performance and accountability of the federal government for the American people. GAO examines the use of public funds; evaluates federal programs and policies; and provides analyses, recommendations, and other assistance to help Congress make informed oversight, policy, and funding decisions. GAO's commitment to good government is reflected in its core values of accountability, integrity, and reliability. |
| **Obtaining Copies of GAO Reports and Testimony** | The fastest and easiest way to obtain copies of GAO documents at no cost is through GAO's website (http://www.gao.gov). Each weekday afternoon, GAO posts on its website newly released reports, testimony, and correspondence. To have GAO e-mail you a list of newly posted products, go to http://www.gao.gov and select "E-mail Updates." |
| **Order by Phone** | The price of each GAO publication reflects GAO's actual cost of production and distribution and depends on the number of pages in the publication and whether the publication is printed in color or black and white. Pricing and ordering information is posted on GAO's website, http://www.gao.gov/ordering.htm.<br><br>Place orders by calling (202) 512-6000, toll free (866) 801-7077, or TDD (202) 512-2537.<br><br>Orders may be paid for using American Express, Discover Card, MasterCard, Visa, check, or money order. Call for additional information. |
| **Connect with GAO** | Connect with GAO on Facebook, Flickr, Twitter, and YouTube. Subscribe to our RSS Feeds or E-mail Updates. Listen to our Podcasts. Visit GAO on the web at www.gao.gov. |
| **To Report Fraud, Waste, and Abuse in Federal Programs** | Contact:<br><br>Website: http://www.gao.gov/fraudnet/fraudnet.htm<br>E-mail: fraudnet@gao.gov<br>Automated answering system: (800) 424-5454 or (202) 512-7470 |
| **Congressional Relations** | Katherine Siggerud, Managing Director, siggerudk@gao.gov, (202) 512-4400, U.S. Government Accountability Office, 441 G Street NW, Room 7125, Washington, DC 20548 |
| **Public Affairs** | Chuck Young, Managing Director, youngc1@gao.gov, (202) 512-4800 U.S. Government Accountability Office, 441 G Street NW, Room 7149 Washington, DC 20548 |

Please Print on Recycled Paper.